Quilting

Quilting
Betty Alfers

Over Fifty Attractive Designs for You to Piece, Appliqué, Embroider, and Stuff

Bobbs-Merrill
Indianapolis/New York

Library of Congress Cataloging in Publication Data

Alfers, Betty.
   Quilting.

   1. Quilting.   I. Title.
TT835.A44   746.4′6   78-55662
ISBN 0-672-52235-7

Designed by Rita Muncie
Manufactured in the United States of America

First printing

To Evelyn Gendel, my dear departed friend
and one of the reasons this book was written
and
To Donald T. Hawthorne, my greatest help
with some of the problem illustrations

Table of Contents

Introduction
Part I: The Basics
1. **Techniques** 13
    Enlarging or Reducing the Design 13
    Making Templates 14
    Selecting Materials 14
    Preparing and Cutting Materials 15
    Piecing 17
    Appliquéing 18
    Embroidering 19
    Stuffing for Accent 21
    Marking the Quilting Lines 22
    Assembling the Layers 22
    Quilting 23
    Finishing the Raw Edges 25
2. **Tools** 28

Part II. The Projects
    In Color 33
3. **Designs for Clothing and Accessories** 41
    Aprons 41
    Skirts 45
    Shirts 48
    Bags 60
    Sandals 68

4. **Designs for Kids** 71
    Bibs 71
    Patches for Jeans 79
    Stuffed Toys 86
    Children's Sleeping Bags 94
    Gingham Flower Quilt 98
    Circus Quilt 101
    Flying Mother Goose Quilt 107
5. **Designs for the Home** 110
    Card-Table Cover 110
    Wall Hangings 114
    Pillows 124
    Pincushions 132
    Christmas Decorations 140
6. **Designs for the Kitchen** 148
    Tea Cozies 148
    Toaster Covers 156
    Cooking Mitts 160
    Pot Holders 165
    Plate Mats 176
7. **Designs for Classic Quilts** 181
    Victoria Green Quilt 181
    Strawberry Quilt 185
    Rob Peter to Pay Paul Quilt 187
    Double Irish Cross Quilt 190
    Whig Rose Quilt 193

Introduction

It was my mother, many years ago, who first brought quilts and the craft of quilting into my life. She began making two Grandmother's Flower Garden quilts. They took her a long time, but she made them well and with a great deal of love, and they are still being used today. One is on a bed in my home and is a favorite resting spot for my dog Tiger; the other keeps my grandsons Kevin and Patrick warm. Little did my mother know how long her quilts would last or what a large and cherished role they would play in my family's life.

Later, when I was a freshman at Smith College, I needed some extra money and found myself a job in a small crafts shop in the village. It was run by a lovely, talented lady from England, and she agreed to teach me all the various crafts while I helped her on Saturdays. She began with quilting, and perhaps because it was the first, it has remained my favorite of all the needle crafts. It was from her that I learned the basics, like making sandpaper templates and how to sew tiny, accurate stitches; but she also taught me much about how to use color properly and how to create new designs. Her taste and talent went a long way toward not only making my college years fun, but providing me with a rewarding pastime and profession for more years than I like to admit to.

Making quilted things has always seemed to me one of the most versatile of hand crafts. You can make small things like toys, pot holders and charming Christmas decorations that take only an hour or so, or you can make large appliquéd wall hangings and intricately pieced full-size quilts. The latter can easily take years, of course, but to me they are years filled with happily spent hours. In this book I've included some of both kinds of projects. Obviously, the big complicated things take more skill and concentration than the simpler ones, but I wanted both the beginners and the more expert among you to find interesting new designs to try your hand at.

Which brings me to one of the most important and enjoyable aspects of making quilted things—not being afraid to experiment with new designs and new techniques. My first design ideas came from children's coloring books. The shapes were simple to copy and fun to make. I also traced the outlines of leaves from different trees—the oak, the maple, the elm, the gum. The colors in the leaves gave me ideas as to what fabrics—print or plain, dark or light tones—to make them out of. As you can see from this book, I'm very fond of animals—giraffes, elephants, lions—and flowers too. But no two people copy nature in the same way; so I hope that after making some of my shapes, you will feel confident enough in your own taste and skill to launch out on your own and try to create some new designs yourself.

Expand your repertoire in other ways too.

Combine appliqué and piecing in the same thing. Or, as I have suggested in many of the projects in this book, add embroidery accents where you think they will look interesting and attractive. Especially on appliquéd figures—a clown, for instance, or a nursery rhyme figure like Mother Goose—embroidered lines on faces and clothes make figures seem almost to come alive. I also like to give some of my work a three-dimensional look by adding stuffing to certain parts of the design. Since I've started stuffing my work, I've begun to look at designs—my own and traditional ones—with a whole new perspective. I hope you will too.

I have only one real caution for you. Making quilts and quilted things has such a long and deservedly treasured history in America that many people, I'm afraid, take the many technical skills involved for granted. I hope you won't. Each step in making even the simplest project is as important as the next, beginning with making an accurate template right down to taking the final stitch when finishing the edges. Since I feel so strongly about this, I have devoted the beginning of this book to telling you exactly how I do each step. I hope you will read this opening section very carefully before making any of my designs. And if, as you follow the directions for an individual project, you are uncertain as to how to manage a certain step, I hope you will refer to the opening section, where I've tried to cover them all in detail. I really believe that if a thing is worth making at all, it is worth making well.

Part I:
The Basics

1. Techniques

Enlarging or Reducing the Design

Working with new designs such as the ones in this book or those you create yourself is one of the great delights in making quilted things. However, unless the design is exactly the right size for your particular needs, you will have to change it—by either reducing or enlarging it. The easiest way I've found to do this is by the square method. Divide the chosen design into 1-inch squares. (The designs in this book have already been diagrammed in this way to make it easy for you.) Next, outline on a piece of paper the total size of the object you want to make; divide this outline into exactly the same number of squares. When this is done, although the number of squares on the paper and on the design are the same, their comparative size will be different. For a larger-sized item, each square will be larger, and for a smaller one, each square will be smaller. Now, working square by square from the original design, make a freehand copy in the corresponding squares on your paper. See Figure 1 of the owl below. You will notice that each corresponding square contains the same amount of the owl; only the size is different.

If you prefer to use graph paper to change the

Figure 1

size of a design, first copy the chosen design onto tracing paper. Then, using dressmaker's carbon paper, copy it onto graph paper; a good size to use is one with four squares to the inch. Now, on another piece of graph paper mark the size to which you wish to reduce or enlarge the design and work freehand, square by square, as described below.

You can use this method equally well when you want to reduce or enlarge only a section of a particular design. For instance, you may wish to use only part of a design intended for something big like a quilt or wall hanging and put it on a small thing such as a pillow cover or pot holder. To do this, count only the number of squares covering the part of the design you want to use, and then follow the instructions above for reducing it or enlarging it to the proper size.

Making Templates

For each different piece of your design, you will need a separate pattern, or template, to use as a guide when cutting out your fabric. I think sandpaper is the best material for templates because it will not slip or shift when the rough side is laid face down on the fabric. Years ago, people often used tin to make templates, and today heavy brown paper, cardboard, even clear plastic is sometimes used. However, I believe sandpaper makes the best template and strongly urge you to use it.

Trace the outline of each piece of your design accurately onto ordinary paper, making sure to add and mark a ¼-inch seam allowance all around if it is not already included. I prefer to add the seam allowance when making the cutting template so I know I won't cut a piece too small. You should also transfer to your paper pattern any accent lines, such as eyes, eyebrows, veins in leaves, et cetera, that you

intend to embroider later. You can do this with dressmaker's carbon paper. After you have cut out all the paper patterns, glue them to the back, or smooth, side of the sandpaper and cut out the permanent cutting templates. Use fine sandpaper for light, delicate fabrics and medium-weight for heavier fabrics. Make sure the dimensions of the sandpaper templates are absolutely accurate, indicating the line for the seam allowance and noting on the top of each template the number of fabric pieces to be cut from it. If a large number of pieces are to be cut from a single template, it's a good idea to make more than one cutting template to ensure complete accuracy when cutting out your fabric. Be sure to discard the first template before the edges become ragged or the corners bent. It is far easier to make a new template than to try to sew irregularly shaped pieces of fabric together.

Selecting Materials

The fabrics I use most for the tops and backings of my quilted articles are good-quality medium-weight cottons—broadcloth, calico, gingham, percale—and cotton-and-polyester blends. These are generally colorfast, preshrunk and washable and are marvelously easy to cut and sew. Occasionally I use other fabrics, such as wool, silk, velvet, rayon and satin. However, these materials are more difficult to work with; they often ravel easily and stretch as you sew them and are usually not washable. For these reasons I would strongly suggest that you use them sparingly, if at all, and then only for purely decorative things such as wall hangings.

The colors and patterns of the fabrics you select play an important role in the final look of any design, so you should choose them with great care. Actually, I find it great fun to experiment with a variety of combinations before I finally make my choices. Your own taste, of course, will play a major part in your selection of fabrics, as will your experience with colors and how they blend together. But don't be afraid to try something unusual once in a while—say, balancing pale, delicate shades with strong, bright colors; or using only two colors, but choosing muted shades of each and placing them against a stark white background. If your quilted piece is to decorate a room, you should consider the colors and patterns already there so that your wall hanging or pillow cover will create an effect but will still blend harmoniously. If it is an article of clothing, make sure the colors selected flatter the wearer. For children's things, bright primary colors—red, yellow and blue—are always good, but for the nursery I am old-fashioned enough to still prefer the palest of pastels.

Don't overlook the effect of patterned fabrics. Not only do they lend a sense of movement and texture to any design, but they also can often take the place of embroidery work or other decorative stitching. Small overall patterns seem to work best in most of my designs, although on occasion I've found a larger geometric pattern surprisingly effective. Fortunately, there are no really hard-and-fast rules for selecting colors or patterns. Follow the dictates of your own eyes, experience and taste. I've done that for years and am generally very well satisfied with the results.

When selecting fabric for the backing, make certain it is of the same quality and fiber content as the fabric or fabrics you have chosen for the top. Backing material is usually plain colored, but there is no reason not to have patterned fabric if it seems appropriate. When choosing plain colors for the backing, pick either an attractive contrast or the same one used for the background of the top.

Batting—sometimes called filler—is used for the middle layer of quilted things. It is widely available in either cotton or polyester.

Cotton was the first material used, and some dyed-in-the-wool traditionalists will use nothing else. Since the cotton batting is usually thinner than the polyester, I feel that it quilts up much thinner and smoother. Polyester, on the other hand, has a finish to it and is lighter and fluffier, which makes it less likely to lump when washed. I prefer polyester batting in the same way that I prefer a refrigerator to an icebox. Both kinds of batting are available in a variety of sizes; the smallest is enough for a crib quilt, and the largest—90 x 108 inches—is fine for a full-sized quilt. Always buy more batting than you will need for a particular project. You can always trim off the excess or use what is left over for a smaller quilted thing or for stuffing.

The loose stuffing which I suggest you use to give added accent to many of my designs is available in convenient small packages. It is made of polyester and is very fluffy. You will soon be able to judge how much to buy for any particular stuffing job.

Preparing and Cutting Materials

Before cutting any fabric, make certain it is colorfast and preshrunk. If in any doubt, wash a small piece as a test. Wash the entire fabric if it shrinks any appreciable amount. Be sure to press all fabrics completely smooth before you mark or cut them. Lay the fabric right side up on a flat surface. To cut out the individual pieces for the design, begin at one side of the material and, moving from left to right, place the sandpaper template on the fabric, rough side down, so its long lines run parallel to the grain of the fabric. The selvedge on many fabrics makes a good guideline. In the case of patterned fabrics or fabrics with a distinct one-way design, make sure you place the template so the design runs the same way every time. Never cut fabric on the bias unless specifically told to.

Trace around the templates with a dressmaker's marking pencil, allowing roughly ⅛ inch between pieces for ease of cutting. Use a light-colored marking pencil for dark-colored fabrics and a dark-colored marking pencil for light-colored fabrics. Do not use an ordinary lead pencil to trace the outline, since such lines will not always wash out. Most of the patterns given in this book have the seam allowance of ¼ inch included in the drawing of the cutting template, but always check on this, and, if it is not included, be sure to add ¼-inch seam allowance at this time. Trace each template the number of times your design requires.

Cut out each piece of the design separately. Once all pieces are cut out, transfer all seam lines and accent lines to each piece individually. For appliquéd designs, you must lay each piece face up on a flat surface. Place a piece of dressmaker's carbon paper on top of it, carbon side down, and then place the marked template on top of that. Now trace all lines on the template. They will now appear on the fabric. For pieced designs, you will want to transfer the seam lines to the wrong side of the fabric. In that case, place each piece face down, place the dressmaker's carbon paper on top of it, and then the template with the seam lines indicated on top of that. Trace the seam lines. They will now appear on the wrong side of the fabric. Once you have cut and transferred all seam and accent lines to each piece, stack them in piles according to shape and color and run a double thread or a large hat pin through them to keep them together.

If your design is to be appliquéd, you will need to cut top background fabric on which to sew it. Press the background material smooth and place it right side up on a flat surface. Check your design for the correct dimensions of the top and mark them on the background fabric with a dressmaker's marking pencil,

making sure you allow ¼ inch all around for finishing the edges. If you are making something fairly large, you may have to piece the top to get enough width. Try to avoid a center seam; it will detract from the overall effect of the design. Instead, use the full width of the material—36, 45 or 48 inches—in the center of the top and make up the rest of the required width by adding strips of equal width on both sides.

Before cutting the backing material, decide how you intend to finish the edges of what you are making. If you plan on self-binding them, you must allow 3 inches all around on the backing fabric. For instance, if the top measures 36 x 36 inches including the ¼-inch seam allowance for finishing the edges, the backing fabric must measure at least 39 x 39 inches. For other methods of finishing the edges—adding bias binding, for instance, or a ruffled edging—the backing should measure the same as the top including a ¼-inch seam allowance for finishing.

If you need to piece the backing, you can do it in exactly the same way as you did for the top. Place the full width of the material in the center and make up the rest of the width by adding equal strips on both sides. However, since the backing usually plays a less prominent role and, indeed, is often not seen at all in things like wall hangings, it can be pieced down the center. This single center seam usually gives you more than enough width.

To cut the batting, lay it on a large flat surface, smooth out any humps or wrinkles, and cut it to the same measure as your top. If it is necessary to piece the batting to get the proper dimensions, here is how to do it. Arrange the pieces of batting on a flat surface, so that their edges meet but do not overlap. Now top-lock the edges together by using large whipstitches, catching first one edge and then the other. (See Figure 2.) Do not pull the stitches too tightly or the edges may begin to overlap. Do this on one side of the batting first,

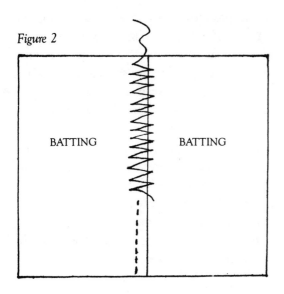

Figure 2

BATTING   BATTING

and then turn the pieces over and do it on the other. This works particularly well with polyester batting, because after the first washing the two edges will fuse together and remain firm.

Piecing

Piecing means the joining of two pieces of material along seam lines. Accuracy is the key to successful piecing. To accomplish this, pin and baste the two pieces together, right sides facing, along the seam line, making sure you match corner points exactly. Using good-quality medium-weight thread (cotton if your fabric is cotton, or polyester if it is a cotton-and-polyester blend), make a line of tiny, even running stitches along the seam line. Begin your stitching with a strong knot, and end it with several small backstitches to make it secure. The color of thread to use is up to you. Traditionally, it is white, but you may prefer to use a matching or blending color for your piecing.

Piecing can also be done on the machine. It is more difficult to control the accuracy of your stitching with machine sewing, especially at corners, but if you baste carefully and stitch slowly, it is often less time-consuming.

After each seam has been stitched, press it with an iron. For straight seams, press them open. Curved seams should be pressed to one side and seam allowances on curved lines clipped at intervals to make them lie flat. Many pieced designs are done in the form of blocks. Be sure you finish one block before you begin another.

When all the blocks for the top are completed, lay them out in the proper order on a smooth, flat surface. Check their placement against the original design and then baste all the blocks together. Be sure all corners line up properly; if necessary, ease some seam lines so they all meet accurately. Begin sewing at the top of one row and continue down it until the end. Use either hand sewing with a tiny running stitch, or machine stitching. When all the blocks have been sewn together, press all seams open and then press the entire top.

Figure 3

Appliquéing

Appliqué is the applying of one piece of material on top of another by sewing. Before you actually begin sewing, however, you must turn under the ¼-inch seam allowance of each piece. Straight edges are no problem; they turn under easily and neatly. Curved edges, of which there are many in traditional appliqué work, are more difficult to handle. To ensure that they lie flat and maintain their desired shape, you must clip the curved edges almost, but not quite, to the seam lines. Sharp curves have to be clipped at closer intervals than shallow ones, and there should be a clip at an indentation such as the point where flower petal curves come together. (See Figure 4.)

Once the curved edges are clipped, fold and press the seam allowance under. The easiest way I've found to do this accurately is to make an extra sandpaper template of each shape to use as a pressing template. This template should not include the ¼-inch seam allowance that was added to the cutting template. After the pressing template is made, lay each fabric piece face down on the ironing board, center the pressing template on the back of it, fold the seam allowance over the edges of the template and press lightly with an iron. Do not use too hot an iron, or it may burn the fabric and sandpaper. Remove the template and baste the folded seam allowance in place. Press again.

Some shapes, particularly the popular leaf form, present special problems. Your folding will be neater if you begin at the point and fold the right-hand wedge in first. (See Figure 5.) Press lightly. Then fold the left-hand wedge over that. Press again. Do the same for the other point, and then press down the curved edges in between. Remove the template, baste the folds in place and press again.

The sharpest curves of all are to be found in the full circle—the usual shape for flower cen-

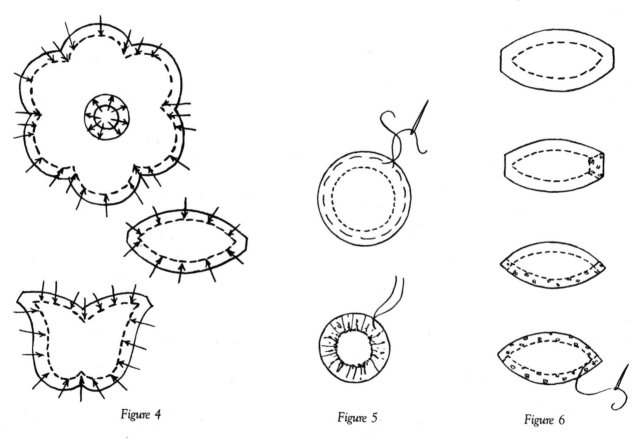

Figure 4   Figure 5   Figure 6

ters. To get a good, smooth shape for a circle, place your round pressing template on the center of the back of the piece of fabric. Trace a line lightly around the edge of it. Now run a basting thread halfway between the traced line and the outer edge. (See Figure 6.) Replace the pressing template and fold the seam allowance over its edges, gently pulling the basting thread to distribute the fullness evenly. Press lightly. Remove the pressing template and baste the folded seam allowance in place. Then press again.

Once the seam allowance of all appliqué pieces has been turned under, place each piece in its proper position on the top background material. This is the only way to be sure that you have all the pieces and that they fit together as they should. Note which pieces overlap others so you will be certain to sew them in place in the correct order. Before appliquéing any piece permanently, baste it to the background fabric in its proper place.

You may do your appliqué work by either hand or machine. I much prefer hand sewing, since I think it is easier, when working with curved edges, to avoid puckering if the fabric is actually in your fingers. For either hand or machine sewing, use a good-quality medium-weight thread (cotton for cotton fabrics and polyester for cotton-and-polyester blends). The traditional hand stitch for appliqué is a tiny, nearly invisible whipstitch. (See Figure 12 and instructions on page 21.) You may also use a small running stitch placed close to the edge of the fold. If you want to appliqué the pieces with embroidery work, see the section on embroidery for suggested stitches.

For machine sewing, use a short running stitch placed close to the folded edge; or, for a more decorative effect, the zigzag or buttonhole stitch will actually outline each shape as you sew. Choose an attractive contrasting color of thread if you wish the machine stitching to serve as an accent.

Embroidering

Since I am personally so fond of embroidery work and feel so strongly that it adds a great deal to the charm of quilted things, I have included many suggestions for ways in which you can accent lines and shapes of particular designs with a variety of embroidery stitches. If you want to try some of them, use a colorfast, washable embroidery floss. The choice of stitch is up to you; however, there are a half dozen or so that are favorites of mine, and you can see how to do them from the following instructions and diagrams.

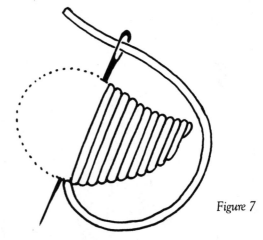

Figure 7

The satin stitch: Used for filling either large or small areas. It consists of vertical stitches placed side by side. Begin from the lower right edge of the motif to be filled and reinsert the needle from top to bottom on each stitch. The only difficulty found will be keeping the outline sharp and clear when the design becomes irregular or curved and the outer edge is larger than the inner edge. Always keep in mind that you must thicken the stitches on the inner edge and space them on the outer edge. If the design widens too much at any point, causing the thread to loosen, divide the area into equal parts and embroider separately. Always direct the stitches to meet at a center V point. (See Figure 7.)

The chain stitch: Most often used as a filling stitch and done in close rows. It adapts easily to scalloped outline work or anything that does not require precision. Working from top to bottom, bring the needle through the fabric to the right side. Hold the thread down with the left thumb, and reinsert the needle as close as possible to the point from which it originally came. Then take a short stitch, bringing the needle out of the fabric a short distance forward and over the thread. Thus, the first link is formed. For the continuing links, the needle is always reinserted at the point where the thread emerged and brought out slightly forward. Keep your thread rather loose and try to avoid too short a stitch. (See Figure 8.)

Figure 8

The stem or outline stitch: Usually used for flower stems and to outline the veining of leaves. Twisted threads are best for this stitch to show clearly its simple construction. The line on which the stem stitch is to be used is rarely straight, as it generally follows curves and circles within the design. Work from left to right, holding the thread above the drawn line on the material, and take short, even stitches from right to left, bringing the needle out on the line the work is to follow. (See Figure 9.)

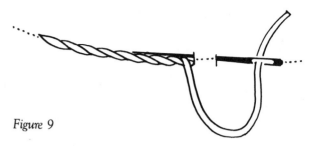

Figure 9

The straight or running stitch: Worked in alternating rows to produce a smooth, uniform effect. It gives a fresh look to many designs with raised textures. It can also be used by itself to get a clear, strong effect. It is usually done following the straight grain of the fabric, if possible. The needle passes under one thread of the fabric and over as many as you want in order to produce the desired effect. (See Figure 10.)

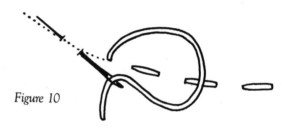

Figure 10

The French knot: Fine for working a monogram or the centers of flowers or as an accent on other designs. Bring the thread up through the fabric. Wrap it over and under the needle once, crossing the beginning thread. Insert the needle in the fabric close to where it came up. Your thread may be used double to produce a larger knot; a larger needle will also do the same thing. (See Figure 11.)

Figure 11

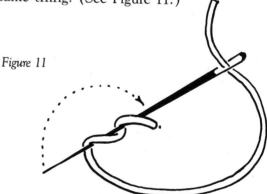

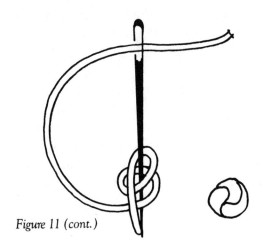

Figure 11 (cont.)

The whipstitch or hemming stitch: Used to finish edges, such as the edges of binding on the quilt, or to appliqué design pieces to the top of your quilted item. Sewing from right to left, the needle catches the folded edge of the hem to the material. Spacing varies according to the type of material being used. (See Figure 12.)

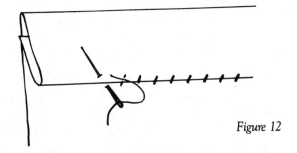

Figure 12

Stuffing for Accent

I very much like to stuff my quilted articles and have been amazed at the difference it makes in the overall effect of so many designs. If you have never done it before, I hope you will try some of my stuffing suggestions and see for yourself how attractive it can be. The only equipment you need is a narrow, relatively sharp pointed instrument such as a knitting needle, a sturdy darning needle or a firm toothpick; and, of course, the stuffing.

Before beginning to stuff, decide which parts of a design seem suitable and whether you will add only a small amount of stuffing or fully stuff the piece. In the flower design on page 48, for instance, I suggest that the center be fully stuffed and the surrounding petals be only lightly stuffed. This makes the center more prominent. Each design, of course, has its own requirements, and your own taste will play a large part in determining where and how much stuffing you choose to do.

You can stuff only appliquéd designs, and usually stuffing is done before you join the top to the batting and backing. If you intend to do any stuffing, do not sew completely around the pieces to be stuffed. Leave an opening through which you can insert the stuffing. The more a piece is to be stuffed, the larger the opening should be.

The technique for stuffing is really very simple. If you are stuffing something small, such as the center of a flower, I suggest using a toothpick for inserting the stuffing. Take a very small ball of loose stuffing, put it on the tip of the toothpick and insert it in the opening. Push the stuffing to the edges of the flower center all around. Continue doing this until the edges are packed evenly and as high as you want. Using your fingers on the outside to move the stuffing around also helps to distribute it more evenly. When the center is packed as firmly as you want, add one more small puff of stuffing for good measure. Now close the opening with a tiny, firm whipstitch. The same technique is used for larger items—say, the head of an animal—but you should use something stronger, such as a knitting needle, for inserting the stuffing and moving it around. Remember that the effect you are trying to achieve is firm roundness, not lumpiness, so be sure you distribute the stuffing as evenly as possible, and always add the extra puff of stuffing just before you close up the opening.

Marking the Quilting Lines

Before assembling the three layers for quilting, you must decide on the pattern for your quilting stitches and mark it on the top. It is the quilting stitches that hold the three layers of material together, and the lines of stitching must be close enough—no more than 2 inches apart at any point—to keep the layers, particularly the batting, from slipping or shifting out of position. Select the stitch pattern for your quilting with care, since it will have a considerable effect on the final look of your quilted project.

One of the simplest and most attractive ways to arrange quilting stitches on appliquéd tops is simply to follow the outlines of your design. Lay your top with all appliqué work, embroidery stitches and stuffing completed on a flat surface, and, using a dressmaker's carbon pencil, mark a line ¼ inch outside of each shape. Never place quilting stitch lines along existing seam lines or on top of stuffed areas of the design; it is too difficult to sew through them. For pieced designs or for appliqué designs in which there is a good deal of open space between shapes you can use a simple diamond-shaped pattern for your quilting stitches. Beginning in the center of the top and using a ruler or T-square and a dressmaker's marking pencil, mark straight diagonal lines to the outer edges. Be certain the lines are no more than 2 inches apart (closer, if you feel the size or design of your top requires it). (See Figure 13.)

If you wish to attempt more elaborate quilting stitch designs, such as a floral or shell motif, perforated or iron-on patterns are available for these designs in needlework shops. Directions for transferring the stitching patterns to your top accompany them.

Assembling the Layers

Before basting the three layers of your quilted article together, make certain that the top is pressed smooth and that the backing and batting are cut and, if necessary, pieced to the proper size. Lay the backing, face down, on a flat surface. Place the batting on top of the backing, smoothing out any bumps or wrinkles. Unless you intend to self-bind your quilted thing, be certain the edges of the batting and the backing are even. For self-binding, there should be 3 inches more of the backing than the batting all around. Now place the completed top on top of the batting, right side up, with all the quilting stitch lines marked. The edges of the batting and the top should be even all around. After making sure

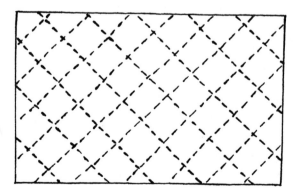

Figure 13: Diagonal quilting lines

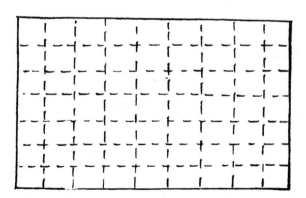

Figure 14: Square quilting lines

the top is smooth, pin it carefully in place through all three layers. Following Figure 15, baste the three layers together. Remember to begin basting in the center and go first lengthwise and then across. Then baste diagonally across the center. Finally, baste around all the sides. Use long, secure stitches and thread of a contrasting color so the bastings will be easy to remove when the quilting is completed.

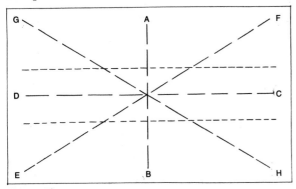

Figure 15

Quilting

Quilting stitches may be done either by hand or by machine. I much prefer hand work. Not only do I find it more fun and vastly more satisfying than machine work; I also think the final product is far superior—stronger, more durable and more attractive to look at. And there is no question that anything you quilt by hand will be much more valuable in years to come. Quilting by machine is, of course, quicker and, if you use a quilting foot, is not difficult even when working on quite large things. I will explain how to quilt both by hand and by machine.

Quilting by Hand

The hand-quilting stitch is a simple, tiny running stitch that begins at the top, goes down through all three layers and then comes back up to the top again. A good rule of thumb is to try to make nine small stitches for each 1 inch of length. They need to be this close together if you want to be sure the three layers are securely fastened. If you are new to quilting or unaccustomed to hand sewing, begin quilting something small; or, better yet, practice on scraps to get the feel of it. Although it takes a long time, years in fact, to become a really expert quilter, you will be surprised at how quickly you pick up the rhythm of the stitch and your quilting becomes quite creditable.

The best needle to use for quilting is a #9-Between; it is about 1 inch in length and fits beautifully in your fingers. I strongly advise using a thimble when you quilt to save your middle finger from too much wear and tear. Choose a matching color thread, in cotton for all-cotton fabrics or polyester for cotton-and-polyester blends. There is no reason to buy special quilting thread. If you like, you can pull your thread over beeswax before beginning to sew; this will give it added strength and help prevent it from snarling as you work. Always begin quilting with a single strand of thread about 12 inches long with a small knot at the end.

There are two good ways to make the quilting stitch. You might try both to see which is easier for you. The first is to insert the needle down through the top, through the batting, and out the backing, and then push it up again very close to the first stitch through all three layers to the top. One hand is always underneath the backing to guide the needle, since the length of the stitch should be the same on both the top and the backing. (See Figure 16 on page 24.) The other way is to take two or three small, even running stitches through all three layers before pulling the needle out. Again, try to make the stitches on the top and those on the back the same length. (See Figure 17 on page 24.)

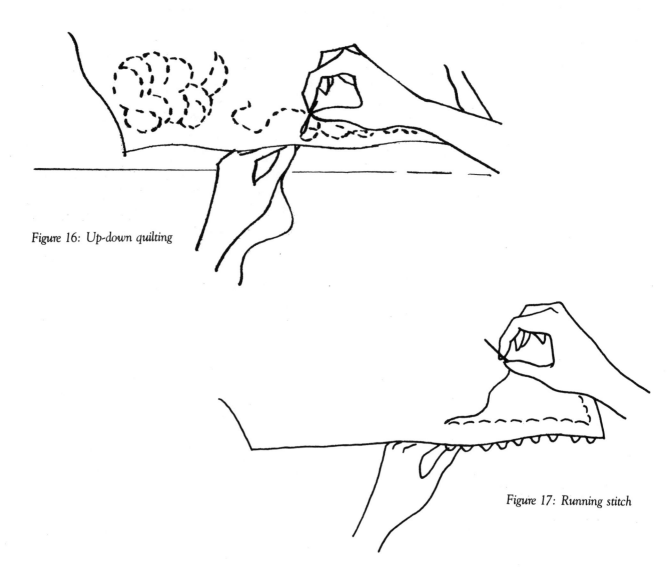

Figure 16: Up-down quilting

Figure 17: Running stitch

Whichever sewing method you choose, you must never allow the knot at the end of your thread to show either on the top or the backing. The way to avoid this is to push the needle up through the backing, through the batting and to the top where you want to begin quilting; now tug very gently on the thread until the knot goes through the backing and is buried in the batting. You may have to tug a few times before the knot disappears from view. Begin sewing at the point where the needle comes out on top. To end your thread, make two small slip knots in it, and then run your needle through the batting and out the top again on the stitching line. Pull gently until the slip knots disappear into the batting, and then clip off your thread close to the surface of the top, allowing the end to slip back into the batting.

Always begin quilting in the center of the top and move from right to left. You can use a quilting frame if you like; it is helpful when you are working on something very large. For smaller things many people like to use a hoop. Either a frame or a hoop keeps the three layers taut while you quilt. I personally use nothing when I quilt, but I always make sure the three layers are basted securely together, and I always work from the center out, no matter what size the article. Your quilting is finished when you have quilted to within ½ inch of the edge on all your marked quilting lines.

Quilting by Machine

A quilting foot makes quilting by machine much easier. Attach it to your machine, set the stitch length for between eight and nine stitches to the inch, and adjust the pressure foot to a lighter tension than normal. Practice the stitch length and tension on scraps before beginning your actual quilting, and adjust them if necessary. Begin all your quilting in the center and work out toward the edges. Diagonal quilting lines are the easiest to stitch on a machine because you are sewing on the bias, which makes it easier to keep flat the area where you are working. As with hand quilting, you have finished quilting when you have stitched within ½ inch of the edge on all your marked quilting lines.

Finishing the Raw Edges

After all the quilting has been completed, it is time to finish the raw edges. There are several ways I like to do this. One of the easiest is simply to whipstitch the top and the backing together along flush, folded seam lines. Another simple way is self-binding. But sometimes I think bias binding, either purchased or the kind you make yourself out of fabric, makes a more attractive finishing touch. I also use ruffles or rickrack, and I like to add cording to the edges of pillow covers, pincushions and pot holders. The size and nature of your quilted

article often dictates how to finish its edges. Although I have suggested how to finish the edges of each design in this book, you may choose whichever way seems most appropriate to you. Here's how to do them all.

Whipstitching Edges

Trim all layers of your quilted thing—top, batting and backing—evenly all around. Be sure to leave a ¼-inch seam allowance. Now fold under the seam allowance on both the top and the backing, and trim any excess batting flush with the two folded edges. Baste the folded edges together so they are flush. Whipstitch the edges and remove the bastings.

Self-Binding

For this method, you will have already cut the backing at least 3 inches larger all around than the top and batting. (See section on preparing and cutting materials, page 15.) Trim the top layer and batting evenly all around, and measure and trim the backing so it is an even 2¼ inches larger all around. If you want a narrower border showing on the top, trim the backing to the desired width, making sure to allow a ¼-inch seam allowance. Fold under the seam allowance on the backing and baste. Bring the folded edge over the batting to the top and pin it in place. Measure to see that the width of the backing showing on the top is the same everywhere. Baste the folded edge in place on the top and, using a small whipstitch, sew the backing in place. Remove the bastings.

Bias Binding

Trim all layers—top, batting and backing—evenly all around. Be sure to leave a ¼-inch seam allowance on the top and backing. Measure all around the edges and add ½ inch for seam allowance. This is the amount of bias binding you will need. If you are using purchased bias binding, sew the ¼-inch seam at the two ends of the strip. Now open up the binding and place one of its edges, wrong side up, along the edge of the top. Pin and then baste the two edges together along the seam line. Sew along the seam line either by hand or machine. Remove the bastings and fold the binding over the edge to the backing of the quilt. With its seam allowance folded under, whipstitch the binding to the seam line on the backing of the quilt.

If you want to use binding made out of strips of your own fabric, be sure to select fabric that is the same quality as that of your top and backing. Choose the width you wish for the binding, double it (the binding shows on both the top and the backing), and add ½ inch for folding under (¼ inch for each side). Measure as you did above to determine the length of the binding. Now cut long bias strips the desired width, joining as many as necessary to get the required length. Attach it in exactly the same way as for purchased bias binding.

Ruffled Edging

A ruffled edging can be made from the same fabric as your top or from an attractive contrasting color of a similar-quality fabric. Decide how wide to make the ruffle and add ¼ inch for a narrow hem and ¼ inch for seam allowance. For the length of the strip, measure all around the edge of the top and double it. If the fabric is lightweight or you want a very full ruffle, triple this measurement. Turn up the narrow hem and sew it. Run a line or two of gathering stitches just inside the ¼-inch seam allowance and pull up the gathers until the strip is the required length. Join the two ends of the strip with a ¼-inch seam. Now trim all layers of your quilted thing—top, batting and backing—evenly all around. Pin and then baste the ruffle to the edge of the top along the seam line, right sides facing, and ease it, if necessary, at the corners. Sew either by hand or machine and remove the bastings. Turn the ruffle to the right side and turn the quilt over. Fold under the seam allowance on the backing. Whipstitch the folded seam line neatly to the seam line of the top where it joins the ruffled edging.

Rickrack Edging

Trim all layers—top, batting and backing—evenly all around. Fold under the seam allowance of the top and baste in place. On the right side of the top, pin and then baste the rickrack close to the folded edge. Using thread the same color as the rickrack, sew the rickrack in place with a running stitch through the center and remove the bastings. Fold under the seam allowance on the backing and baste it flush with the folded edge of the top. Neatly whipstitch the two edges together. Remove the bastings.

Cording

Measure all around the outside edges of your quilted item. Add 1 inch to this measurement. This is the amount of cording you will need. You can either purchase color-coordinated cording or make your own so it will match the pillow cover or whatever you are trimming. To make your own, first determine the size of the casing you will need. It should be 2 inches wider than the size of your cord. For example, if your cord measures 1 inch, your casing should be 3 inches wide. The casing will be made from bias strips of your fabric sewn together to measure at least 1 inch longer than the outside edges. Fold the joined bias strips, wrong sides together, around the cord. Using a zipper foot attachment, stitch close to the cording, but not right up against it. After your cord has been encased or you have purchased cording, place the pillow cover, right side up, on a flat surface and lay the cording along its edges. Pin and then baste the edges together. Using your zipper foot attachment, sew the cording to the top of the pillow cover along the seam line. Now take the back of the cover and place it on the top of the cover top, right sides together. The cording should now be between the two layers. Pin and then baste the edges of the top and the back together. With the zipper foot pressed up against the rounded part of the cording, sew along the seam line. Remember, however, to leave one side open in the case of a pillow cover (you have to insert the pillow form) or an opening large enough to insert stuffing in the case of a pincushion or pot holder. Clip the curves and corners and turn right side out. After you have inserted the pillow form or the stuffing, whipstitch the opening closed.

2. Tools

Before you start any of the projects in this book, it is a good idea to have on hand all the tools and other equipment you will need. Everyone, of course, has favorite ways of doing things and special tools that make it easier for the way she likes to work; for this book and the projects I've included in it, I find the following things most useful.

Graph paper: This can be used when you are reducing or enlarging a design; 4 squares per inch is a good size. You can, of course, make your own squared paper to the required size.

Sandpaper: To make templates, purchase a good grade of sandpaper with a grit similar to the weight of the fabric on which it will be used, that is, a fine grade for delicate fabrics, a medium grade for most other fabrics.

Marking materials: Choose whichever means— dressmaker's marking pencil or dressmaker's carbon paper—is appropriate for marking your fabric. You can use an ordinary lead pencil for marking paper when you change the size of a design or for making templates, but do not use it on fabric. It does not always wash out.

Tape measure, ruler, yardstick or T-square: A tape measure is used for measuring curved lines and a straight-edged ruler is used for measuring straight ones. A T-square can be used for marking diagonal quilting lines.

Scissors: You will need a pair of 5-inch embroidery scissors to work on appliqué pieces and, as you quilt, a larger pair of sharp scissors for cutting out fabrics, and an old pair of scissors for cutting paper and sandpaper patterns. Never use scissors with which you cut fabric for cutting paper; it ruins the cutting edge.

Pins and pincushion: Use a good grade of rustproof dressmaker's pins and a pincushion filled with sand to keep the pins sharp.

Needles: You actually need only one kind of needle—a #9-Between. With it you can do all your appliqué and piecing work, as well as your quilting. A crewel embroidery needle is necessary for any embroidery work you do. The size depends on the kind and width of embroidery floss you choose.

Thread: Purchase a good grade of medium-weight cotton or polyester thread. For all-cotton fabric use all-cotton thread; for cotton-and-polyester blends use polyester thread. The color of thread depends on your choice of fabric. Be sure to have some contrasting colors on hand for basting.

Embroidery floss: Colorfast, washable embroidery floss of three strands is needed for any embroidery work you wish to do.

Thimble: This is virtually a must if you are going to quilt by hand. Choose a plastic one that fits comfortably on your finger.

Iron and ironing board: You will need to press fabrics before cutting them and to press seams as you piece and before you appliqué.

Quilting frame or hoop: These are necessary only if you are working on larger-sized items, and not even then if you have basted the layers together securely.

Sewing machine: You don't really need one unless you intend to do part or all of your stitching by machine.

Narrow, pointed instrument: A knitting needle, a strong toothpick or a darning needle to insert stuffing will be needed.

Beeswax: You can pull your sewing thread over beeswax to give it strength and help prevent snarling as you quilt.

PART II:
THE PROJECTS

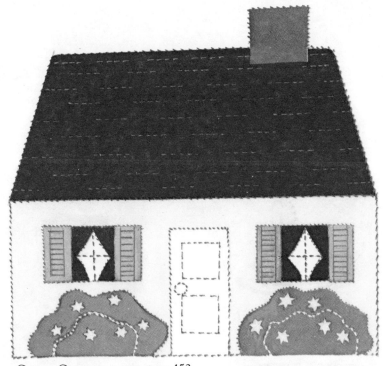

Canary Cottage tea cozy, page 152.

Half-Moon knitting bag, page 61.

Farmyard Scene work shirt, page 54.

Heart pincushion, page 136.

Soldier bib, page 71.

Giraffe sleeping bag for child, page 94.

Gingham Flower quilt for crib, page 98.

Circus quilt, page 101.

Flying Mother Goose quilt, page 107.

Star of the West plate mat, page 176.

Dresden Plate plate mat, page 178.

Girl with a Flowerpot cooking mitt,
page 163.

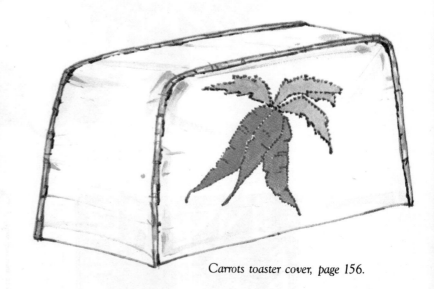

Carrots toaster cover, page 156.

Bird of Paradise
Christmas decoration, page 143.

Victoria Green quilt, page 181.

Bear's Paw pillow, page 124.

Pine Tree pillow, page 128.

Whig Rose quilt, page 193.

Rob Peter to Pay Paul quilt, page 187.

3. Designs for Clothing and Accessories

Aprons

A simple apron made from plain fabric can be turned into something quite special if you sew an attractive design on it. Here are two easy ones to appliqué and stuff. You can use them for regular-length aprons or for long ones that cover an at-home skirt. The important thing is to make the designs big enough. In my directions I suggest enlarging them, but you might want to make them even bigger, particularly if you are putting them on a long apron.

Apple

Size:
7½ x 9½ inches

Materials:
Apron
¼ yard of red polished cotton, 36 inches wide
Scraps of green material
Embroidery floss
Small amount of loose polyester stuffing

Directions:
1. Make templates for each of the three different parts of the design. Enlarge them by using 2-inch squares, rather than the 1-inch squares shown in Figure 18. You will need to cut one of each part. Transfer seam and accent lines to each piece.
2. On the apple (#1), embroider both the

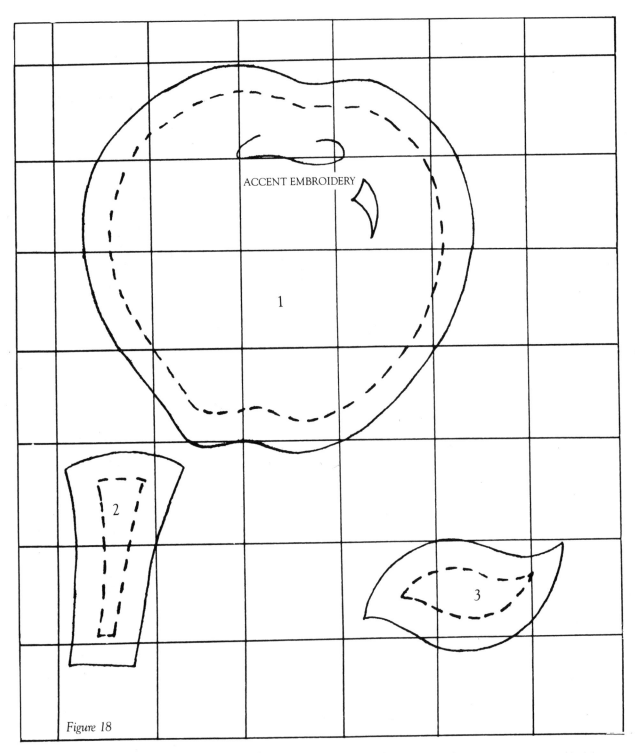

ACCENT EMBROIDERY

1

2

3

Figure 18

accent mark and the semicircle at the bottom of the stem in the satin stitch.

3. Appliqué the apple (#1) first, leaving an opening on one side to stuff. Stuff it very fully and close up the opening. Next, appliqué the stem (#2) at the top of the apple. Leave an opening at the top and stuff it lightly. Close up the opening. Finally, appliqué the leaf (#3) at the side of the stem. Leave an opening and stuff quite fully. Close up the opening.

Mushroom

Size:
10 x 10½ inches

Materials:
Apron
¼ yard each of two different materials, 36 inches wide, for the mushroom
Embroidery floss
Small amount of loose polyester stuffing

Directions:
1. Make templates for each of the two different parts of the design. Enlarge them by using 2-inch squares, rather than the 1-inch squares shown in Figure 19. You will need to cut one of each of the parts. Transfer seam lines to each piece.
2. Check the illustration at right and note the position of the grass line below the mushroom. Embroider this in place on the apron, using the stem stitch.
3. Appliqué the base (#2), making sure it rests on, but does not cover up, the embroidered grass line. Leave the top of the base open and stuff it lightly. Close up the opening.

Appliqué the top of the mushroom (#1), leaving an opening at the top. Stuff the top of the mushroom very fully and close up the opening.

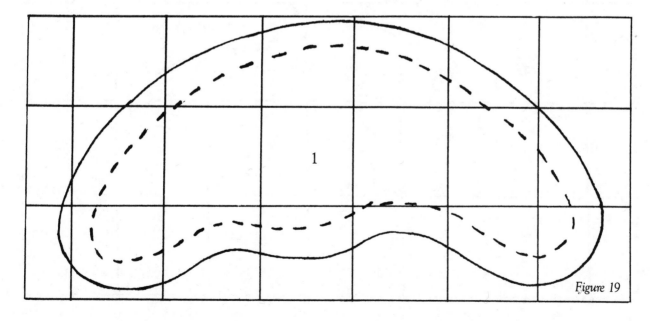

Figure 19

Figure 19, cont.

Skirts

Here are two easy ways to add color and excitement to simple long skirts. Both designs look equally attractive on shorter skirts too; but, whatever the length of skirt you choose, I would suggest making both designs out of paper first and checking their size before cutting the designs out of fabric. The poppy, particularly, should be large enough to make a real splash. It might well be that you will have to enlarge it. The poppy appliqué is special in another way as well; its petals are not completely sewn down, so you must make not only a top, but a backing as well, for each of them. As for the strawberry border, the lower width of your skirt will determine how many strawberries you will need to make a complete border. Measure both your skirt and the strawberry and decide how far apart to place them. Then you can figure out how many to cut.

Poppy

Materials:
Skirt
¼ yard of red or orange soft material, 36 inches wide
Scraps of green and black material
Embroidery floss (optional)
Small amount of loose polyester stuffing

Directions:
1. Make templates for each of the six different parts of the poppy design. Remember that the petals (#1 and #2) are not completely sewn down, so you must make a top and a backing for each of them. Mark on each template how many to cut and from which fabric. You will need to cut two of the top petal (#1) from the red or orange fabric, ten of the lower petal

(#2) from the red or orange fabric, two of the leaf (#3) from the green scraps, four of the short stem (#4) from the green, two of the long stem (#5) from the green, and one of the center (#6) from the black. Transfer seam lines to each piece.

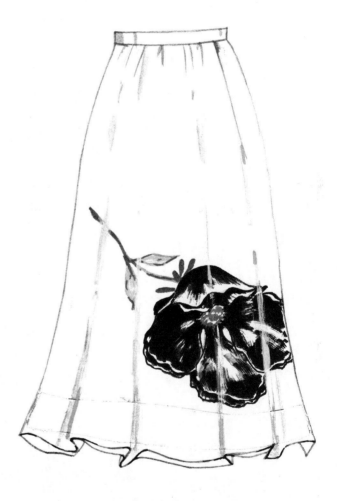

2. First make the complete petals. Take the two top petals (#1), place them right sides together and baste around the seam lines. Leave enough of an opening to turn them. Sew on the basted line, remove the bastings and turn right side out. Slightly stuff the top petal and close up the opening. Do the same for the ten lower petals (#2), making sure you close up the opening after stuffing each of them.

3. Check the illustration on page 45 to see where to place the two long stems (#5) and the leaves (#3). Appliqué all of these in place on your skirt. If you would like to stuff the leaves lightly, leave an opening for this. When all the leaves have been stuffed, close up the openings.

4. Again checking the illustration for placement, pin the petals to the skirt, beginning with the top petal (#1) and then adding the lower petals (#2). Note that they all flow from the center. Now pin the center (#6) in place, and adjust the others if necessary. Appliqué the top curve of the top petal (#1) in place first. Next, appliqué the center (#6), and, finally, catch one or two of the edges of the other petals. Do not sew them completely down. Fluff the petals a little to be sure the stuffing is evenly distributed. Now appliqué the short stems (#4) in place at the top of the top petal (#1).

5. As an added accent you could embroider several large French knots in the center (#6), or just add some straight black lines in the center done in the chain stitch.

Strawberries

Materials:
Skirt
¼ yard of plain red or red paisley material, 36 inches wide
Scraps of green material
Embroidery floss (optional)
Small amount of loose polyester stuffing

Directions:
1. Make templates for each of the two different parts of the design. Decide how many strawberries you will need to make a complete border. This is the number of stalks (#7) and

strawberries (#8) you will need to cut. Transfer seam lines to each piece.

2. If you are using plain red fabric for the strawberries and would like to give the look of seeds, embroider several small French knots around the bottom of each berry.

3. Now appliqué all the strawberries (#8) in place, making sure they are spaced evenly around the skirt. Leave an opening at the bottom of each for stuffing later. Now appliqué the stalk (#7) in place on top of each strawberry.

4. Stuff the strawberries very fully and firmly and close up the opening.

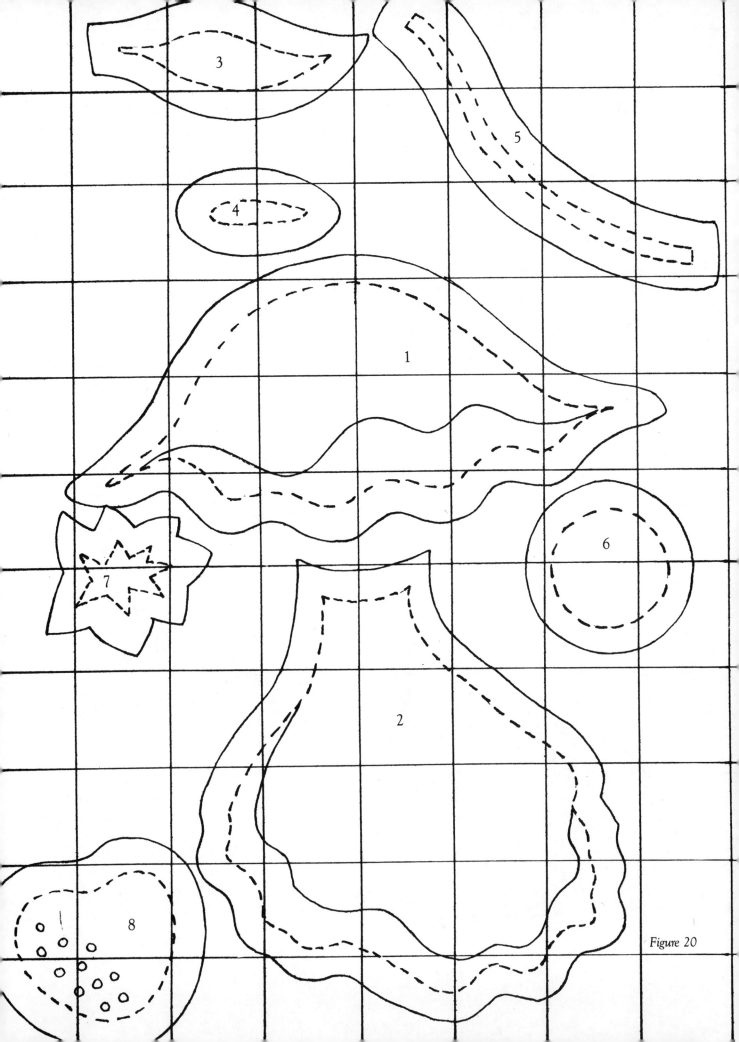

Figure 20

Shirts

Here are some designs you can use to jazz up ordinary work shirts. They are fun to do and, depending on your time and energy, can be as elaborate or as simple as you like. I find that once I get started I usually fill up the whole shirt, but it will look just as attractive if you decide to use only part of the design. A note on caring for appliquéd shirts: I suggest washing them by hand, putting them in the dryer for just a few moments to remove any excess water

from the stuffing and then hanging them on the line to dry. Also, don't press the designs too firmly or they will flatten out.

Flower

Materials:
Work shirt
Scraps of material
Embroidery floss
Small amount of loose polyester stuffing
3 yards of cotton eyelet trim

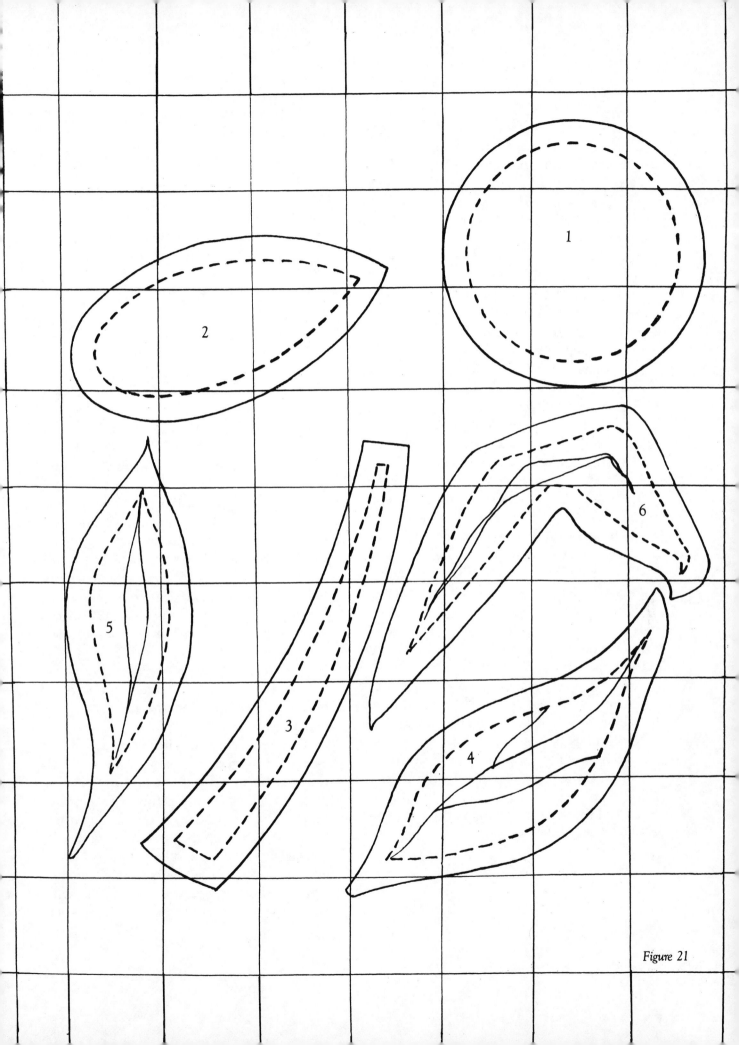

Figure 21

Directions:

1. Make templates for all parts of each flower. The size of the templates will depend on the size of your shirt. It might be a good idea to make them out of flexible paper first to judge whether you should reduce or enlarge them. Mark on each how many pieces to cut and from which fabric. The daisy design consists of six parts. Decide how many daisies you wish to appliqué. For each you will need to cut one of the center (#1), eight of the petal (#2), two of the stem (#3), one of leaf #4, one of leaf #5 and one of leaf #6. The template diagrams for the daffodil can be found in Figure 45 on page 116. For each daffodil, you will need to cut one of the flower (#1), one of the small leaf (#2), one of the small petal (#3), two of the large petal (#4), one of the leaf (#5), one of the stem (#6) and one of the bending leaf (#7). Transfer seam and accent lines to each piece.

2. Do the following embroidery work before you begin to appliqué. On the daisy the center (#1) can be filled in entirely with the satin stitch or with many small French knots. The veins of the various leaves can be done in the stem stitch. On the daffodil do the stamens in the satin stitch and the veins of the petals and leaves in the stem stitch.

3. Study the illustration on page 48 to decide where you will place your flowers. Do them in the following order: Appliqué the stems and leaves of each flower first. Leave an opening at the bottom of each stem and the side of each leaf for stuffing lightly. Close up the openings. Next, appliqué the centers and stuff them a little more fully. Close up the openings. Finally, add the petals and stuff lightly. Close up the openings.

4. Add the eyelet trim around the collars and cuffs of the shirt.

Ladies with Balloons

Materials:
Work shirt
Scraps of material
Embroidery floss
Small amount of loose polyester stuffing
Small buttons
Tiny beads
Cotton balls from curtain trim
Bias binding, narrow
Grocery string
3 yards of cotton eyelet trim

Directions:

1. Make templates for each different part of the design. Study the illustration opposite. You will note that there are two different ladies— one with a face, and one with no face, just a large hat. Decide how many ladies of each kind you wish to appliqué on your shirt. For each lady with a face, you will need to cut one face, one gathered hat, one jumper, one blouse, one skirt, two legs, one purse, two hands and one balloon. For each lady with no face, you will need to cut one large flat hat, one jumper, one blouse, one skirt, two legs, one purse, two hands, one or two pigtails and one balloon. Transfer all accent and seam lines to each piece.

2. The only embroidery work to be done before you appliqué is on the face. Use one strand of embroidery floss and the chain stitch to make the eyelashes.

3. Decide where you will put each lady on your shirt; I alternated them on mine. Study the illustration again to see how the different parts of each figure fit together. First appliqué the legs. Leave the tops open, stuff them lightly and close up the opening. Turn up the bottoms of the skirts and hem—the skirts will not be sewn down at the bottom—and then appliqué the tops and the sides of the skirts only. Appliqué the jumpers, but leave them

free at the upper sides and tops in order to slip the blouse underneath. Appliqué the blouse in place underneath the jumper, and then appliqué the sides and the tops of the jumpers. Appliqué the hands at the bottoms of the sleeves, leaving a small opening to stuff lightly. Close up the opening. Appliqué the purses to one hand. Leave the bottoms open, stuff lightly and close up the openings.

4. Appliqué the face to the lady who gets one.

Leave the top open. Now sew one small bead to each side of the face for the earrings and several around the neck for the necklace. Add buttons down the front of the jumper. Stuff the face lightly and close up the opening. Gather the hat by sewing a line of gathering stitches on the wrong side. Turn the hat to the right side, and sew on a cotton ball in the center. Appliqué the hat in place, tilting it slightly to one side.

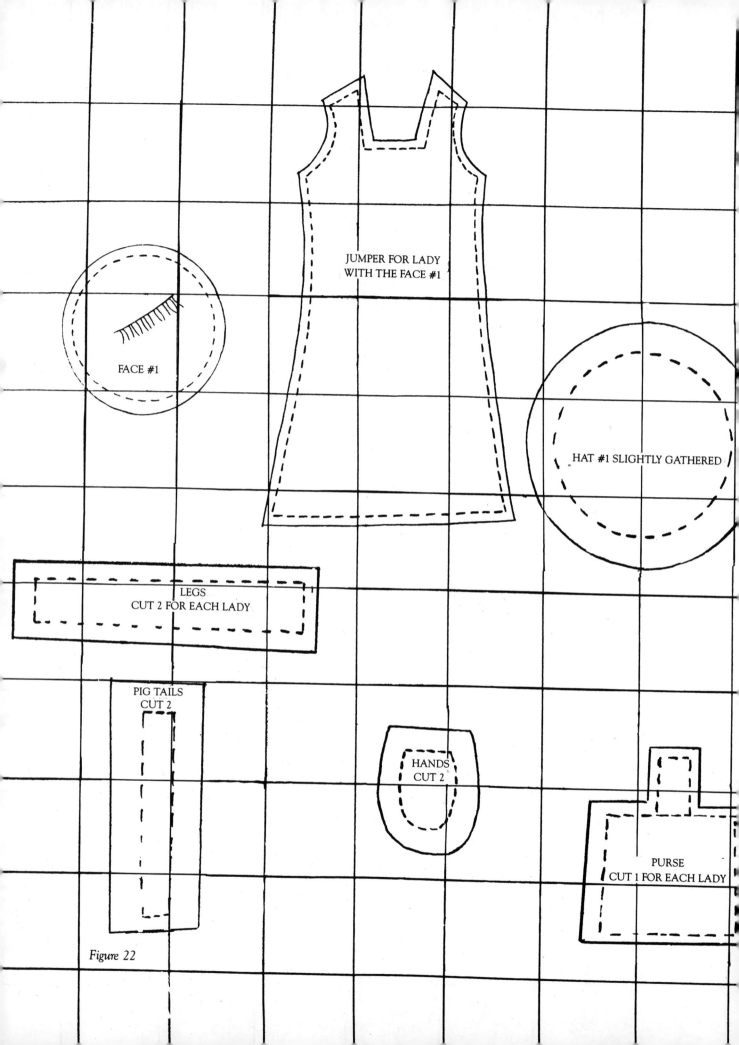

FACE #1

JUMPER FOR LADY
WITH THE FACE #1

HAT #1 SLIGHTLY GATHERED

LEGS
CUT 2 FOR EACH LADY

PIG TAILS
CUT 2

HANDS
CUT 2

PURSE
CUT 1 FOR EACH LADY

Figure 22

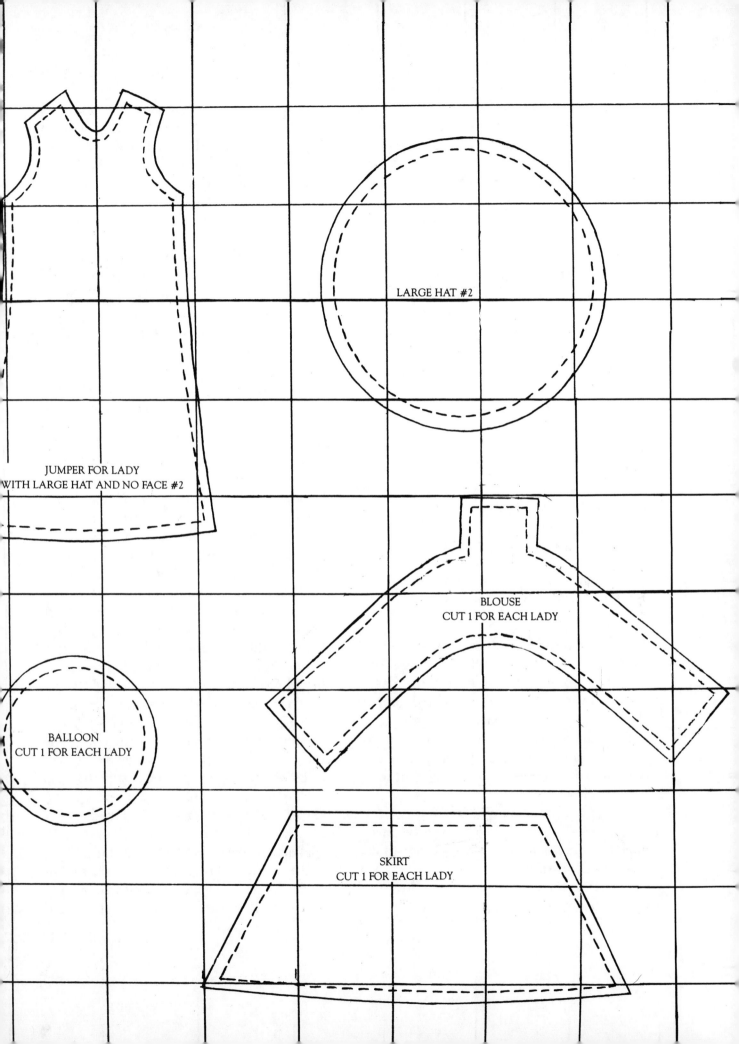

JUMPER FOR LADY
WITH LARGE HAT AND NO FACE #2

LARGE HAT #2

BALLOON
CUT 1 FOR EACH LADY

BLOUSE
CUT 1 FOR EACH LADY

SKIRT
CUT 1 FOR EACH LADY

5. For the lady with no face, sew a cotton ball to the center of her hat and appliqué the hat in place. Appliqué either one pigtail down the center back or two pigtails on either side of the hat. Make small bows from narrow bias tape and appliqué them to the pigtails.

6. Appliqué the string for each lady's balloon—see the illustration for length and placement—by taking tiny tacking stitches along its entire length. Appliqué the balloon at the end of the string and leave the top open. Stuff very fully and close up the opening.

7. Add the eyelet trim around the collars and cuffs.

Farmyard Scene

Materials:
Work shirt
Scraps of material
Embroidery floss
Small amount of loose polyester stuffing
3 yards of cotton eyelet trim

Directions:
1. Make templates for all parts of the design. Since this is a rather complicated design, you may choose to leave one or more of the figures off your shirt. You will cut one of each part of the design, unless you choose to repeat parts such as the fence or the body of the cow, as shown in the illustration opposite; then you will cut two. Transfer all seam and accent lines to each piece.

2. There is a fair amount of embroidery work to be done—some of it before you begin to appliqué and some after. Here is what to do first: On the barn sides, do the horizontal accent lines in the chain stitch in a contrasting color. For all the rest of the lines—the window, the large V, etc.—use the satin stitch. On the side building, fill in the window with the satin stitch. On the silo, the top should be outlined with the chain stitch. On the fences, use the chain stitch to indicate the posts and the wood grain. On the pig, use the chain stitch for all the accents, but wait until he is on the shirt to do the tail. On the duck, use a French knot for his eye and a chain stitch for the rest of the lines. The cow requires the most embroidery work of all. Do all the spots on the body in the satin stitch and the hooves in the chain stitch. The tail will be done later. On the cow's face, use the chain stitch for all the accent lines, but wait till later to do her horns and the hay in her mouth. On the scarecrow, use the chain stitch for the band on his hat, the eyes, the nose, the mouth and other accent lines shown on his coat and pants. Use French knots, however, for the buttons as well as for the eye of the crow on his sleeve.

3. Study the illustration opposite and decide where you want to put the different parts of the design on your shirt. Begin by appliquéing the two parts of the fence and lightly stuff each. Close up the openings. Appliqué the mailbox on top of the fence and stuff fully. Close up the opening. Embroider the flag on the mailbox in the satin stitch in a contrasting color. Appliqué the barn and stuff lightly. Close up the opening. Add the side building next, and then the silo. Stuff both of these lightly and close up the openings. Appliqué the cow's body next. Stuff it lightly and close up the opening. Embroider the tail at the end of the cow in the chain stitch. Appliqué the head of the cow and leave an opening to stuff the head and ears lightly. Close up the opening. Embroider the hay in her mouth and the horns at the top of her head in the chain stitch. Appliqué the pig and stuff him very fully. Close up the opening. Use the satin stitch to embroider his tail. Appliqué the scarecrow, beginning with his pants. Stuff them lightly and

Appears in color on page 33

close up the opening. Now appliqué both his feet. Embroider the pole between his legs and the grass near his feet in the satin stitch. Appliqué his coat and stuff lightly. Close up the opening. Add the hands. Appliqué the crow to his sleeve and stuff lightly. Close up the opening. Embroider the crow's feet in the satin stitch. Appliqué the scarecrow's head, leaving the top open for stuffing. Appliqué the neck in

place. Stuff the head and close up the opening. Appliqué his hat, stuffing it lightly and close up the opening. Finally comes the duck. Appliqué his body. Stuff it fully and close up the opening. Add the bill and stuff it lightly. Close up the opening. Appliqué the duck's feet.

4. Add the eyelet trim around the collars and cuffs.

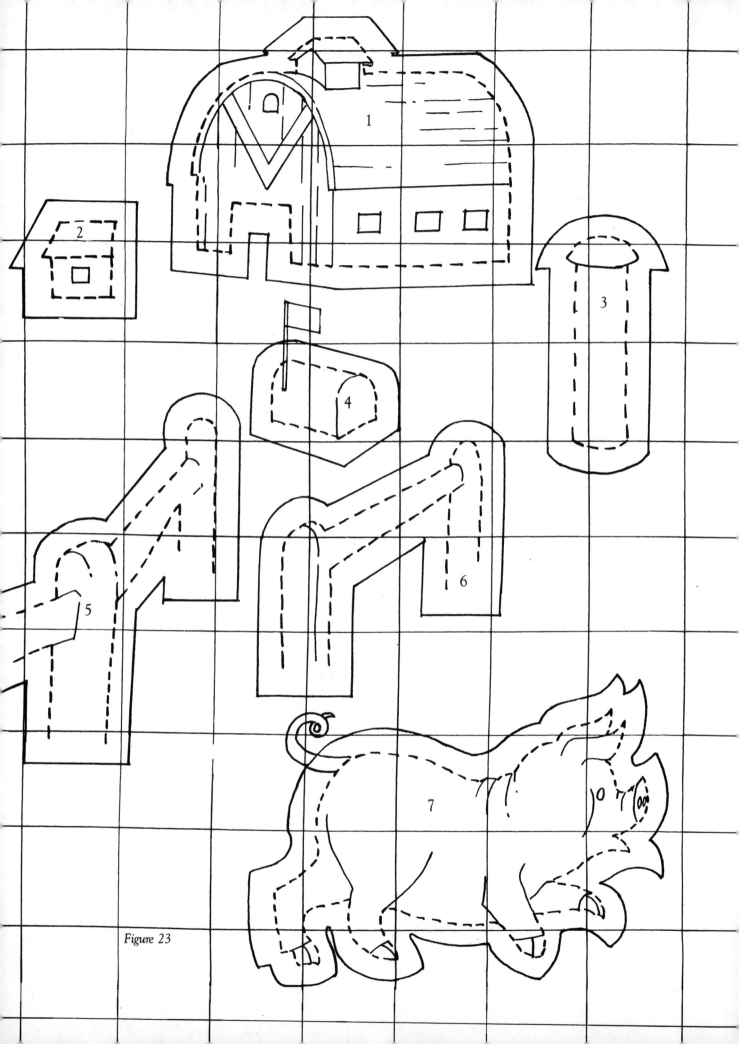

Figure 23

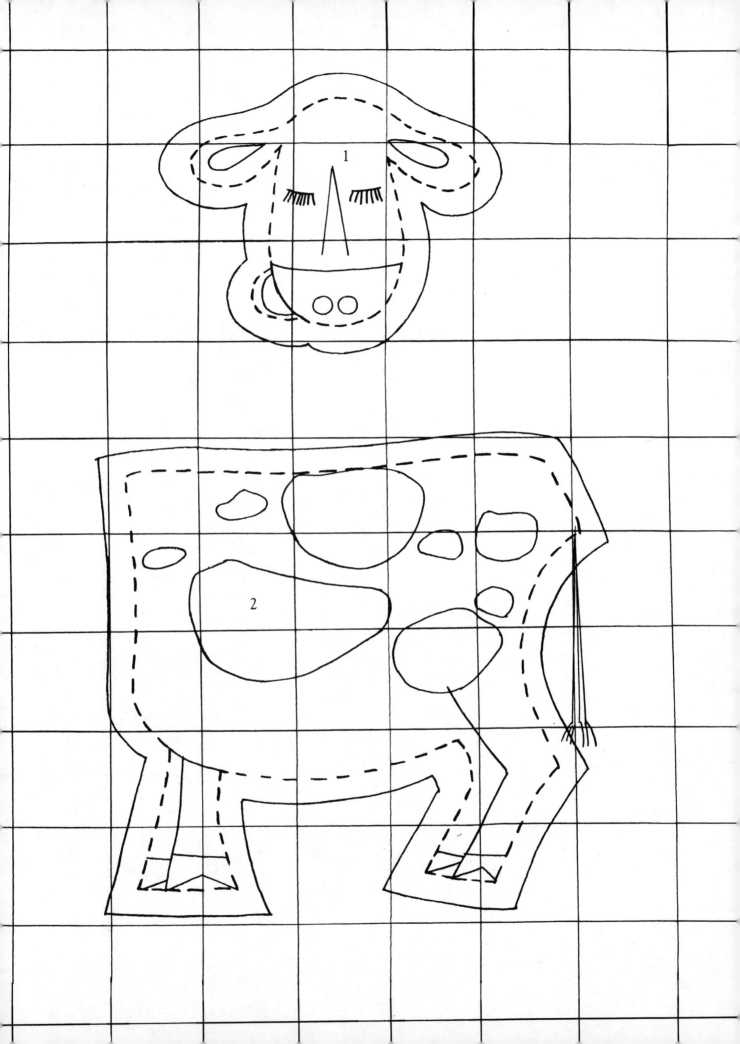

Figure 23, cont.

Bags

Here are designs for three different carrying bags. The patchwork tote bag is a marvelous way to use up a quantity of small pieces of fabric. Since it is made out of rows of 2-inch squares, it is very easy to vary its size; simply change the number of squares either across or down. The knitting bag with its half-moon crescents in a variety of print or plain fabrics slips easily into slotted wooden handles, saving you the trouble of making straps. And the shoulder bag and change purse can easily be appliquéd in designs other than the daisy motif in the illustration on page 64.

Patchwork Tote

Size:
14 x 14 inches

Materials:
Scraps of plain-colored and print cotton material
1 yard of lining material, 36 inches wide
Small roll of batting
3 yards of cotton cording, ¼ inch wide
4 bone drapery rings, 1 inch in diameter

Directions:
1. Make a template that measures 2½ inches square. Mark a ¼-inch seam allowance on it. Using this, you will need to cut ninety-eight squares from a variety of scraps for the bag. Decide on the length of the handles. For two 16-inch handles you will need to cut sixteen squares and for two 22-inch handles you will need to cut twenty-two squares. Transfer seam lines to each piece. You will also need to cut two pieces of lining fabric and one piece of batting, each measuring 14½ x 28½ inches. Mark a ¼-inch seam allowance on all three.
2. First join the ninety-eight squares for the

outside of the bag. Begin by piecing fourteen squares down in a row. Continue piecing rows until you have seven of them. Place the seven rows side by side on a flat surface and first baste and then sew the rows together, making sure corners meet exactly. Press all seams open.

3. To make the handles, piece the remaining squares together in strips just one square wide. Make two rows the length you have chosen for your handles. For a 16-inch handle you will join eight squares in one long strip and eight in another. For a 22-inch handle you will join eleven in one long strip and eleven in another. Press all seams open.
4. Take each strip and fold it in half lengthwise, right sides together, and first baste and then sew along the seam allowance. Turn the strip right side out and press. Pull the cotton cording, doubled, through the handle

strip and trim off the excess. Fold under the seam allowances at both ends of the handles and whipstitch the folded edges together. The handles will be attached to the inside of the bag after it is quilted and lined.

5. Make quilting lines on the patchwork bag. I suggest marking them ¼ inch from each seam line on every square.

6. Baste the patchwork bag, the batting and one of the lining pieces together. Quilt all the marked lines and remove all bastings.

7. Now fold the patchwork bag in half, right sides together, at the bottom of the seventh row. Baste together along the seam lines on the outside edges. Sew them very securely, taking a few extra stitches at both top edges to reinforce them. Trim off any excess batting and turn the bag right side out.

8. Take the other piece of lining and fold it in half, right sides together. Sew along the seam allowances on its long outside edges.

9. Tuck this lining into the patchwork tote and tack it lightly to the bottom and both sides of the bag.

10. Turn under the seam allowances on both the top of the tote bag and the lining and whipstitch the folded edges together all around the top of the bag.

11. Now attach the bone rings, two on each side, about 1 inch below the top edge on the inside of the bag. Sew the rings securely at the bottom.

12. Attach the ends of the handles to the bone rings by folding the ends over the tops of the rings. Whipstitch the handles to the rings.

Half-Moon Knitting Bag

Size:
14 x 14 inches

Materials:
1 yard of white or off-white material, 36 inches wide
1 yard of lining material, 36 inches wide
½ yard of pink material, 36 inches wide
½ yard of light blue material, 36 inches wide
¼ yard of yellow material, 36 inches wide
¼ yard of light green material, 36 inches wide
¼ yard of dark blue material, 36 inches wide
Small roll of batting
Pair of slotted wooden handles, 12 inches long (available at some art and needlework stores or by mail from Jacmore Co., 36 West 25th Street, New York, New York 10010.)

Appears in color on page 33

Directions:
1. Make a template for the knitting bag by using the outside edges of Figure 24 on page 62 as your guide. Enlarge it by using 2-inch squares rather than the 1-inch squares as shown in Figure 24. Using this, you will cut one piece from the white material, one from the batting and two from the lining material. Note that all of these are cut on the fold of the material. Transfer all seam and marked lines to each piece.

2. Now make templates for each of the half-moons. Again, you will enlarge the figure by

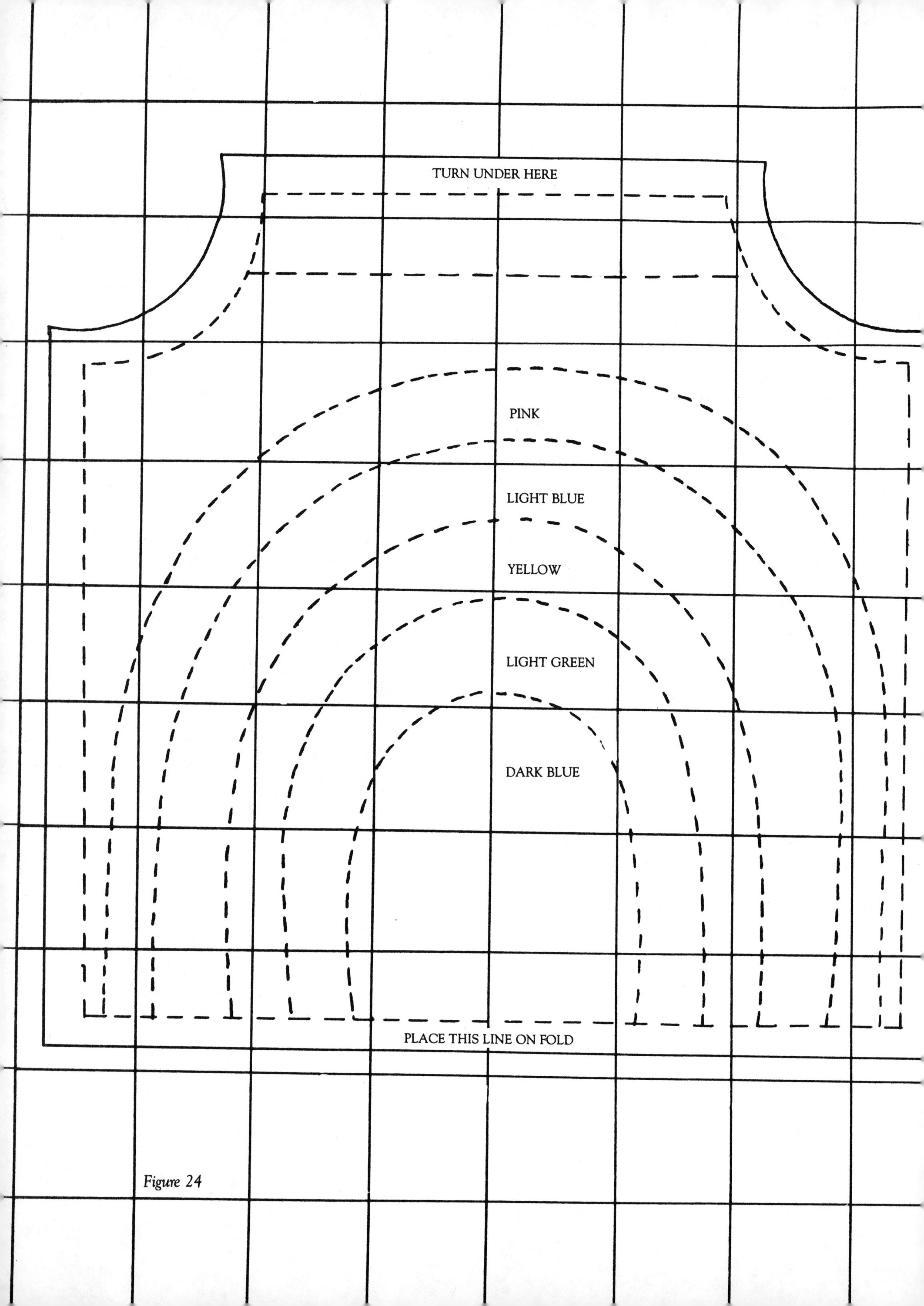

TURN UNDER HERE

PINK

LIGHT BLUE

YELLOW

LIGHT GREEN

DARK BLUE

PLACE THIS LINE ON FOLD

Figure 24

using 2-inch squares rather than 1-inch squares as shown. When making the templates, be sure to add the required ¼-inch seam allowance on both the outside and inside curves. You will need to cut one piece with each template from the color noted on the figure, and I suggest cutting them on the bias to make them easier to work with. Transfer seam lines to each piece.

3. Beginning at the bottom of the front of the knitting bag—the fold line indicates the bottom of the front—and appliqué each half-moon in turn. Start with the dark blue one and continue until you reach the pink one. Be sure to keep the lower edges in line as you work. If you prefer to appliqué the pieces by machine, use a zigzag stitch.

4. When all the half-moons are appliquéd, mark quilting lines ¼ inch from all the curved lines on the front. For the back of the bag, you could mark the same lines as those on the front or simply use a diamond pattern.

5. Baste together the knitting bag, the batting and one piece of the lining.

6. Quilt all marked quilting lines. Remove the bastings.

7. Fold the quilted bag on the fold line, right sides facing. Baste along the long outside edges until you reach the top curved edges. Sew along the basted seam allowances, but do not sew the curves. Remove bastings and turn the bag right side out.

8. Fold the other piece of lining material on the fold line, right sides facing. Baste and sew along the outside seam allowances until you reach the top curved edges. Do not sew along the curves.

9. Tuck the lining into the knitting bag and tack it lightly to the bottom and both sides of the bag.

10. Fold under the seam allowances on the top curves of both the lining and the outside of the bag and whipstitch them together neatly.

11. Slip the top raw edges of the top of the bag through the slots of the wooden handles, turn

under the seam allowances and whipstitch the handles securely in place.

Daisy Shoulder Bag and Change Purse

Size:
Shoulder bag: 13½ x 11 inches
Change purse: 5 x 3 inches

Materials:
1 yard of plain-colored material, 36 inches wide
½ yard of lining material, 36 inches wide
½ yard of Pellon®
Scraps for the flower design
Small roll of batting
3 yards of cotton cording, ¼ inch wide
2 bone drapery rings
Short chain or length of covered round elastic to attach the change purse
2 large snaps (optional)

Directions
1. Make templates for each of the five different parts of the design. Enlarge them by using 2-inch squares rather than the 1-inch squares shown in Figure 25 on pages 65–67. Mark on each the number of pieces to cut and from which fabric. For the shoulder bag you will need to cut four of the bottom of the bag (#1)—one from the plain fabric, one from the Pellon, one from the lining fabric and one from the batting. You will need to cut four of the bag (#2)—one from the plain fabric, one from the Pellon, one from the lining and one from the batting. You will cut only one of the flower design (#3) from scraps. For the change purse you will need to cut four of the purse (#4)—one from the plain fabric, one from the Pellon, one from the lining fabric and one from the batting. You will also need to cut one of the flower design (#5). Transfer all marked lines to each piece. For the shoulder strap, cut a strip of plain material 2½ inches wide and either 16

inches or 22 inches long, depending on how long you want the strap. Mark a ¼-inch seam allowance on the strip.

2. Make the shoulder bag first. Begin by embroidering the center of the flower in the stem stitch. Appliqué the flower in the center of the top flap of the bag (#2). Leave an opening on one petal for stuffing later.

3. Mark quilting lines on both the shoulder bag and the bottom of the bag in evenly spaced diagonal lines.

4. Baste together the shoulder bag (#2), its batting and the piece of Pellon. Also, baste together the shoulder bag bottom (#1), its batting and its piece of Pellon.

5. Quilt all marked quilting lines on both the bag (#2) and the bottom (#1).

6. Now place the bottom of the shoulder bag (#1) on top of the lower part of the shoulder bag (#2), right sides together, and baste along the outside seam allowances. Sew along the bottom and up both sides, reinforcing your stitches at both ends. Remove bastings and turn the bottom of the shoulder bag right side out.

7. Now join the two pieces of lining cut from #1 and #2 at the bottom edges, right sides together.

8. Fold under the remaining raw edges of both the shoulder bag and its lining. Tuck the bottom of the lining into the bottom of the shoulder bag and tack along the bottom and sides. Now baste together the top flap of the shoulder bag and the top flap of the lining along the folded edges and whipstitch together. Do the same for the top of the bottom of the shoulder bag.

9. Fold the top flap of the shoulder bag down and stuff the flower design very fully. Close up the opening.

10. Make the shoulder strap by folding the long 2½-inch strip of fabric in half lengthwise, with right sides together. Stitch along the ¼-inch seam allowance, turn to the right side and press. Pull the cording, doubled, through the inside of the strap and trim away any excess. Turn under the seam allowances at both ends of the strap and whipstitch together.

11. Sew the bone rings at either end of the shoulder bag. Slip the ends of the strap around the rings and whipstitch in place.

12. To make the change purse, first embroider the flower (#5) with the stem stitch. Then appliqué it onto the center of the top flap of the change purse (#4). Leave an opening on the side for stuffing later.

13. Mark quilting lines on the front of the change purse in the same pattern you used for the shoulder bag.

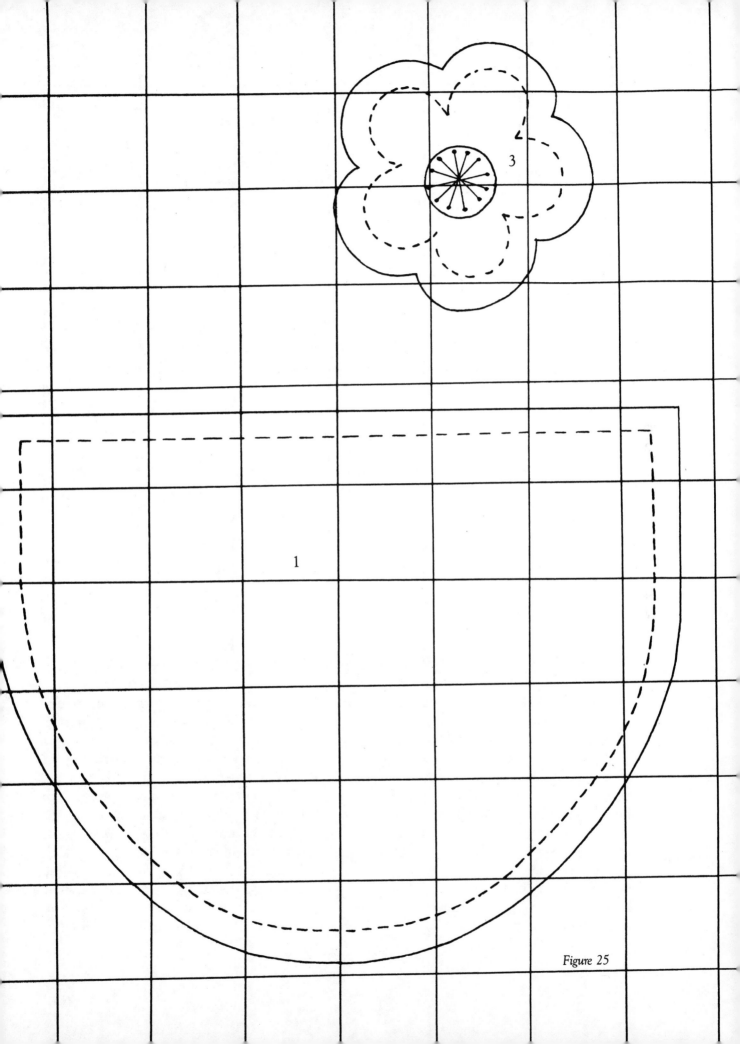

3

1

Figure 25

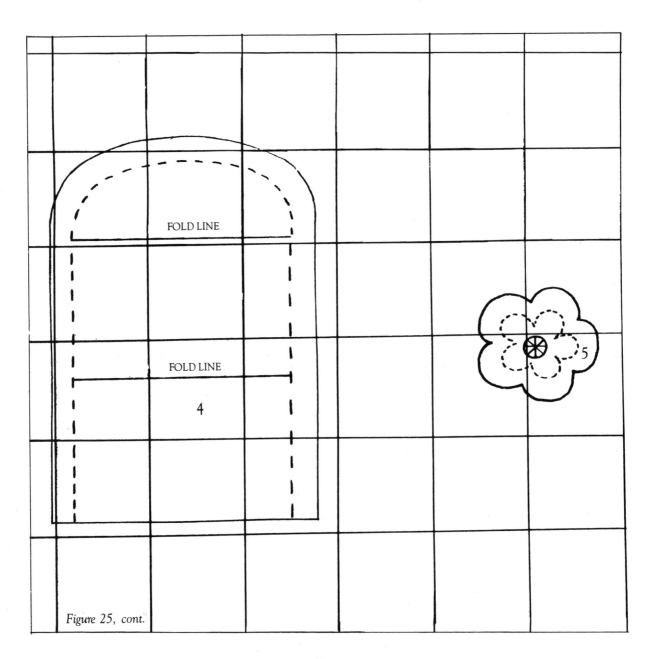

FOLD LINE

FOLD LINE

4

5

Figure 25, cont.

14. Baste the change purse, batting and Pellon together in the same way as for the shoulder bag. Quilt all the marked quilting lines.

15. Fold the change purse along the lower fold line with right sides facing. Baste and then sew along the outside seam allowances, making sure to take a few extra stitches at the top of both sides to reinforce them. Now turn the bottom right side out.

16. Take the piece of lining, fold it on the lower fold line, right sides facing, and sew along the outside seam allowances as you did for the shoulder bag.

17. Tuck the lining inside the change purse, tacking it at the bottom and along the sides. Fold under all remaining seam allowances on both the change purse and the lining and whipstitch together.

18. Fold down the top flap. Now stuff the flower very fully and close up the opening.

19. First sew one end of the chain or round elastic to the change purse and then sew the other end to the inside of the shoulder bag.

20. To close the change purse and the shoulder bag more securely, you can attach large snaps to the undersides of the top flaps.

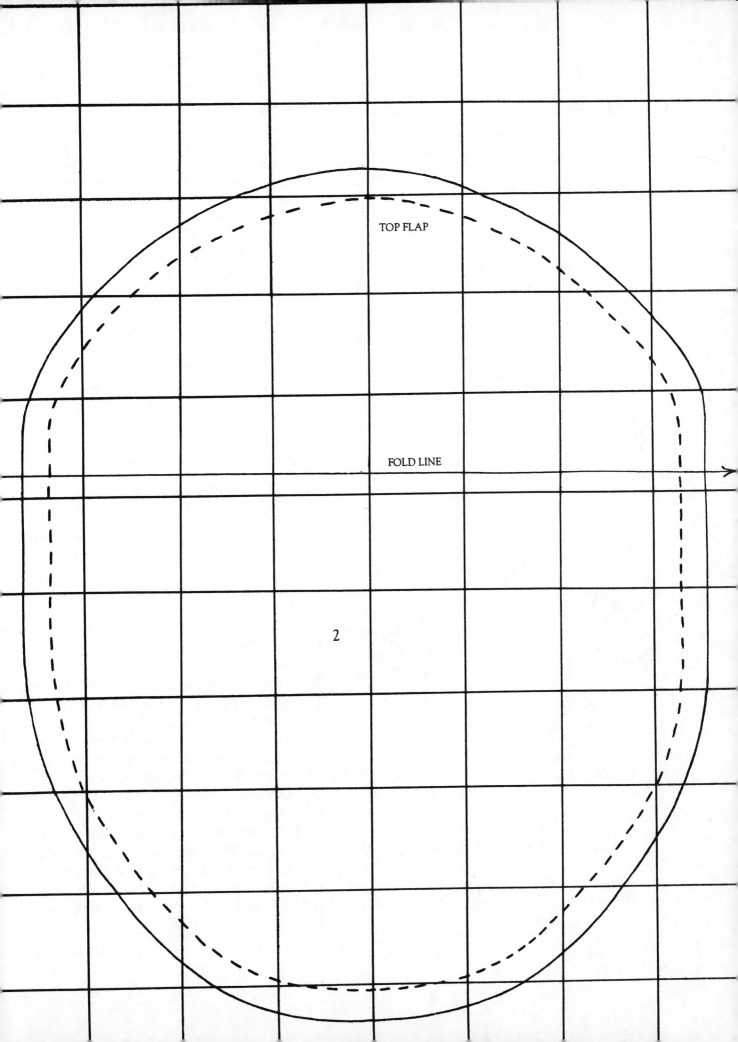

TOP FLAP

FOLD LINE

2

Sandals

Here is a way to brighten up old exercise sandals whose soles are still perfectly good but whose tops are not so new looking. All you do is cut out new tops, using the pattern I've given or removing your old sandal top and tracing around it. Then appliqué a colorful design on them before attaching them to the sandals. To give the top more body, use a fusible web fabric between the top and the lining. And most important of all, never use the old tack holes when tacking the new sandal top in place. Although I've given you template patterns for only one design, there are many in this book that would look terrific on sandals—any of the jean patch designs, for instance.

Materials:
Exercise sandals
¼ yard of plain-colored material, 36 inches wide
Scraps of material for the design
¼ yard of fusible web material, such as Stitch Witchery
Embroidery floss (optional)
16 upholstery tacks

Directions:
1. Make a template for the sandal top, either by using the pattern given (#1) or by tracing around the old sandal top. Note that the template shows only one-half of the top, and all pieces cut from it must be cut on the fold of the material. If you use my pattern, make it first in flexible paper and try it over your instep for size. Make any adjustments in the size before cutting your sandpaper template. You will cut four of the top (#1) from plain-colored material—two for tops and two for lining—and two from the fusible web fabric. Transfer seam lines to each piece.
2. Make templates for each of the four different parts of the flower design. Mark on each how many to cut and from which fabric. For two sandal tops, you will need to cut two flowers (#2), four leaves (#3), two flower centers (#4) and two stems (#5). Transfer seam lines to each piece.
3. First, appliqué the center (#4) to the center of the flower (#2); then appliqué the flower (#2) to the center of the top. If you would like to stuff the flower lightly, leave an opening and stuff. Close up the opening. Next, appliqué the stem (#5). Finally, appliqué the leaves (#3) in place on either side of the stem. Leave an opening on one side and stuff them lightly. Close up the opening.
4. Any extra flowers and leaves on the top can be embroidered, if you wish. Use a satin stitch for the flower centers and leaves and a stem stitch for the stems.
5. When all appliqué and embroidery work is completed, press under the outside seam allowances on both sandal tops and lining. Trim the fusible web fabric to just a fraction of an inch smaller than the tops and lining.
6. Place the lining face down on the ironing board, place the trimmed fusible web fabric on top of it, and then place the sandal top on top of that, face up. Set the iron to the temperature suggested in the directions that accompany the

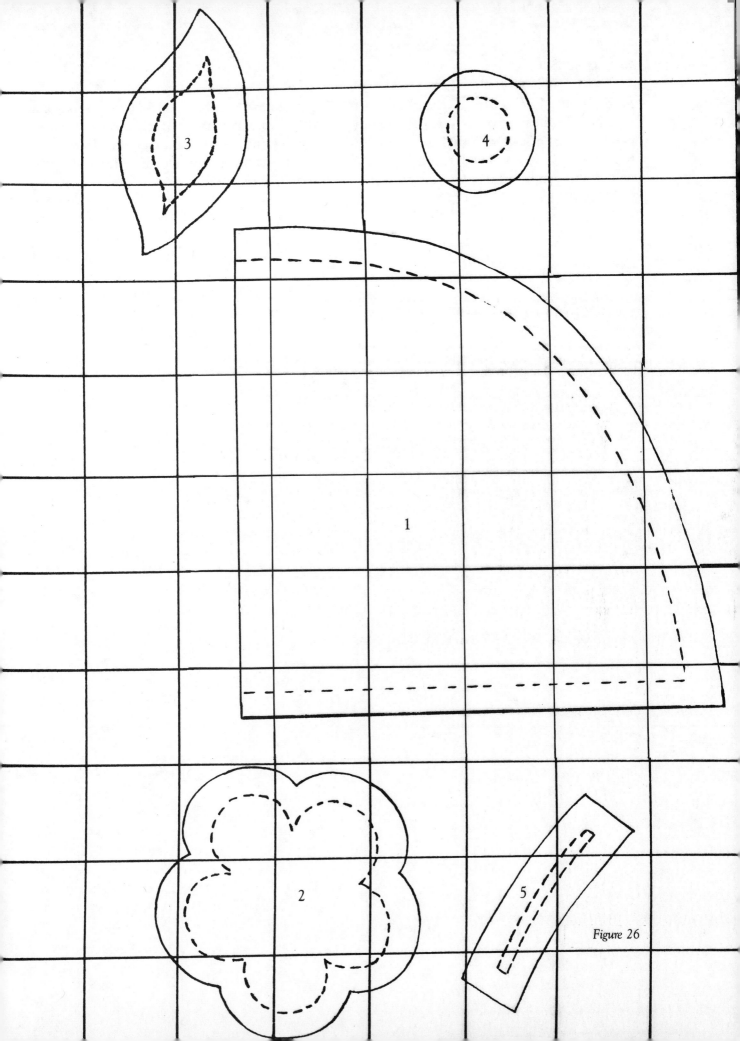

3

4

1

2

5

Figure 26

fusible web fabric and press the three parts together. Be sure to go over the edges carefully, making sure no seam allowances show. Now the three pieces are fused together permanently and can be attached to the soles.

7. Remove the original sandal tops if you have not already done so. Attach the new ones by hammering four tacks on each side. Remember not to hammer the tacks into the old holes; they will not hold.

4. Designs for Kids

Bibs

Here are four different designs that I like to use on babies' bibs. They are easy to make out of scraps of material and are, of course, completely washable. There is no quilting involved, since I suggest using purchased bibs. These designs, enlarged, also look attractive on children's sunsuits, sun dresses or pinafore aprons.

Soldier

Size:
6 inches tall

Materials:
Purchased bib, 7 x 9 inches
Scraps of black and yellow material
Embroidery floss
Small amount of loose polyester stuffing

Directions:
1. Make templates for each of the five different parts of the soldier. Cut one of each. I would suggest cutting the hat (#1) and the pants and boot (#4) from black fabric and the rest from yellow fabric. Transfer seam and accent lines to each piece.

Appears in color on page 34

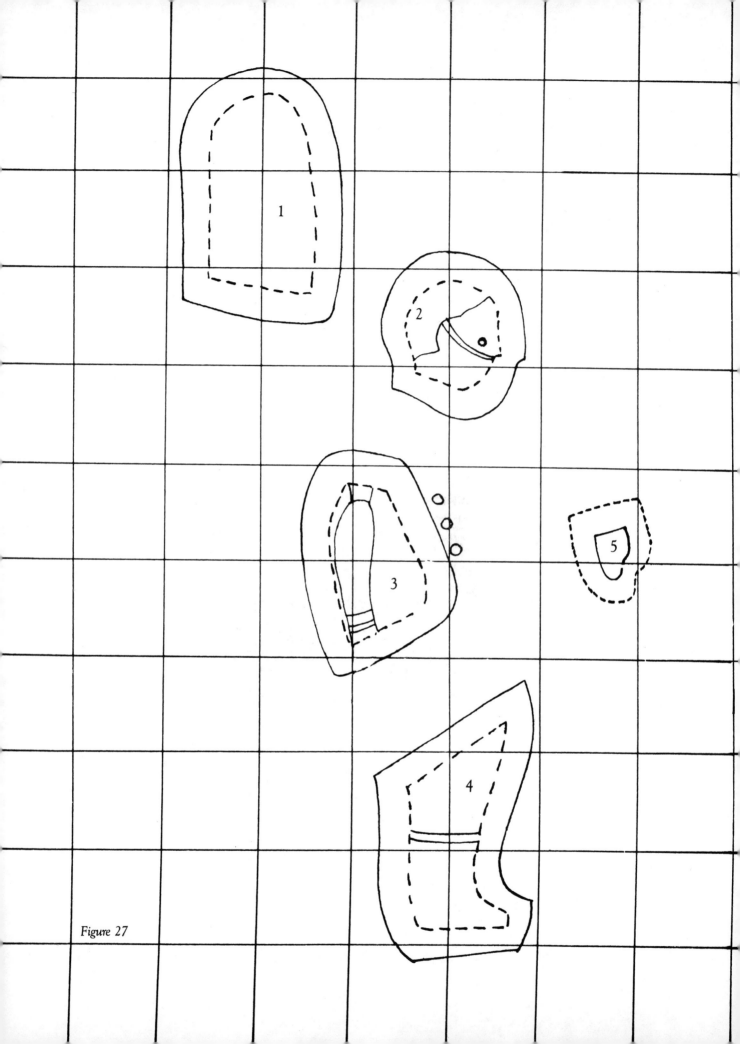

Figure 27

2. Some embroidery work should be done before you begin to appliqué. On the head (#2), work a French knot for the eye and use the satin stitch for the hair and the band under the chin. On the coat (#3), use the chain stitch to outline the shoulder epaulet and the cuff; on the pants (#4), use the satin stitch for the boot line.

3. Study the illustration on page 71 to see where each piece of the design should be placed. Appliqué the hat (#1) first, leaving the bottom open so you can slip the head in place. Next, appliqué the head (#2) and then stuff the hat fully and close up the opening. Now appliqué the coat (#3), leaving the bottom open. Slip the pants (#4) in place at the bottom of the coat and appliqué it, leaving the lower edge open. Appliqué the hand (#5) in place at the bottom of the coat. Now slightly stuff both the coat and the boot and close up the openings.

4. Embroider the peak on the hat in the satin stitch and the four buttons at the side of the coat in large French knots, making sure you space them evenly.

Boy with a Fish

Size:
3¼ x 5½ inches

Materials:
Purchased bib, 7 x 9 inches
Scraps of material
Embroidery floss
Small amount of loose polyester stuffing

Directions:
1. Make templates for each of the five different parts of the design. Cut one of each and transfer seam and accent lines to each piece.

2. Some embroidery work should be done before you begin to appliqué. On the hat (#1), use the chain stitch for the accent lines on the top. On the head (#2), work a large French knot for each eye and use the satin stitch for the mouth. On the body (#4), work several small French knots to give the effect of a design. On the fish (#5), use the chain stitch in a contrasting color of floss to give the effect of scales.

3. Study the illustration below to see where each piece of the design should be placed.

Appliqué the body of the boy (#4) in place first. Next, appliqué the fish (#5), leaving an opening on the outside so you can stuff the fish lightly. Close up the opening. Now appliqué

Figure 28

the head (#2) in place. You will notice on the illustration that there is hair on each side of the head. Embroider this now, using the satin stitch. Next, appliqué the hair (#3) on top of the head. Finally, appliqué the hat (#1) in place.

Girl with a Bird

Size:
5½ x 2½ inches

Materials:
Purchased bib, 7 x 9 inches
Scraps of material
Embroidery floss
Small amount of loose polyester stuffing

Directions:
1. Make templates for each of the nine different parts of the design. Cut one of each except for the pigtail (#3), of which you will cut two. Transfer seam and accent lines to each piece.
2. Some embroidery work should be done before you begin to appliqué. Work the eyes on the head (#2) in French knots and the mouth in the satin stitch. On the bird (#9), use the chain stitch for the wing and a small French knot for the eye.
3. Study the illustration at right to see where each piece of the design should be placed. Appliqué the head (#2) first, leaving openings at each side to slip the pigtails in place. If you wish to stuff the head slightly, leave an opening at the bottom as well. Next, appliqué the hair (#1) in place at the top of the head. Slip the pigtails (#3) into place and appliqué. Now stuff the head if you like and close up the

opening. Embroider the bows at the bottom of the pigtails with a satin stitch. Next, appliqué the body (#4), leaving the bottom open to slip the skirt into place. Appliqué the skirt (#8) and close up the opening. Now appliqué the arm (#5), leaving the bottom open to slip the hand into position. Appliqué the hand (#6),

leaving the top open for stuffing. Stuff the hand from the top and the arm from the bottom and then close up both openings. Now appliqué the shovel (#7) in place. Finally, appliqué the bird (#9), leaving the stomach side open, and stuff, using a toothpick so you can get the stuffing into the bill and tail section. Close up the opening.

Figure 29

Elephant

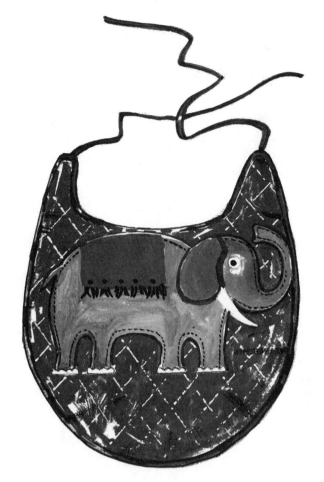

Size:
5½ x 3 inches

Materials:
Purchased bib, 7 x 9 inches
Scraps of gray, yellow and white material
Embroidery floss
Small amount of loose polyester stuffing

Directions:
1. Make templates for each of the four different parts of the elephant. Cut one of each. I would suggest cutting the elephant body (#1) and the ear (#3) out of gray polished cotton, the blanket (#2) out of yellow and the tusk (#4) out of white. Transfer seam and accent lines to each piece.
2. First appliqué the blanket (#2) to the

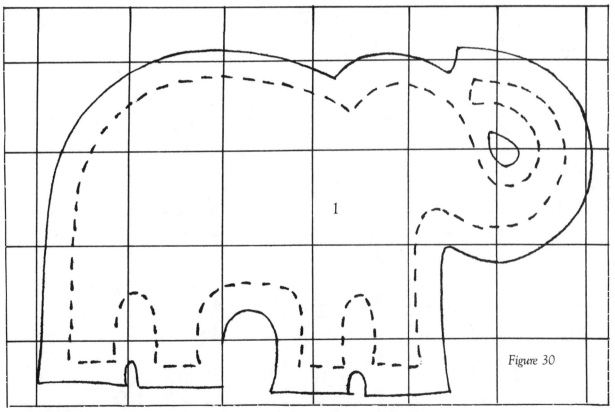

1

Figure 30

elephant body (#1). Work the holes for the fringe in small French knots and the fringe itself in the satin stitch. Now appliqué the elephant body (#1) to the bib, leaving the top of the back slightly open. Stuff the body and legs lightly and close up the opening. Appliqué the ear (#3) in place on the elephant, leaving the bottom open to slip the tusk (#4) in place. Appliqué the tusk (#4) in place and leave an opening on the long curved side. Now stuff the ear slightly and close up the opening. Then stuff the tusk fully and close up the opening. Finally, work a large French knot for the elephant's eye.

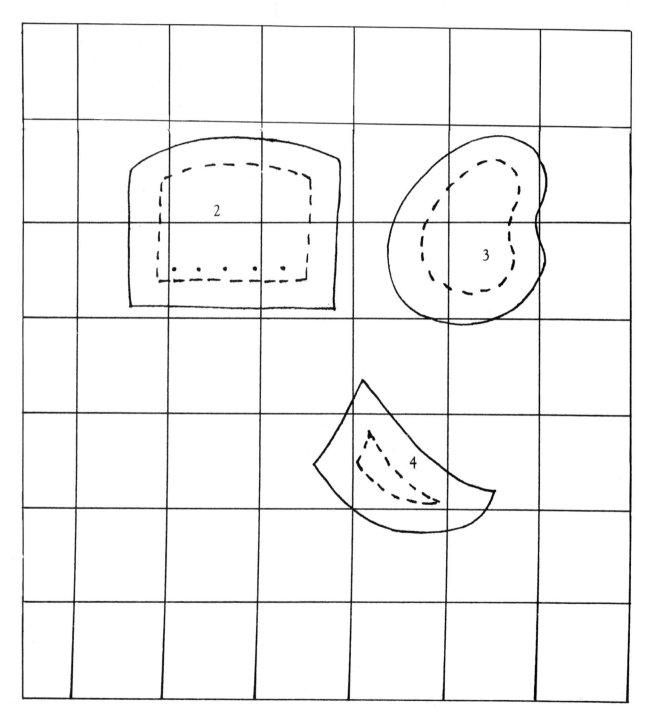

Patches for Jeans

Since kids' jeans are forever wearing through at some place or other, it is a good idea to have lots of different ways to patch them up. These four designs are favorite ones of mine; teen-age friends liked them so much they put them on brand-new pants! All the designs are stuffed, which means you have to make a lining for them. But this is simple to do, once you have completed the patch and its embroidery work.

Monkey

Materials:
Scraps of plain-colored material
Embroidery floss
Small amount of loose polyester stuffing

Directions:
1. Make a template for each of the six different parts of the design and mark on each how many to cut and from which fabric. You will need to cut one of the head (#1), one of the inner head (#2), two of the ear (#3), two of the inner ear (#4), one of the bottom circle of the head (#5) and one of the mouth (#6). Note on the ear templates (#3 and #4) that you must reverse the template when marking its second outline on the fabric. This way the ears will point in the right direction. Transfer seam and accent lines to each piece.
2. Before assembling the patch, embroider both the eyes and eyebrows on the inner head (#2) in the satin stitch. Embroider the nose on the bottom circle of the head (#5) and the inner mouth on the mouth (#6) in the satin stitch.

3. Appliqué the inner ear (#4) in position on the ear (#3). Next, appliqué the ears (#3) to the sides of the head (#1). Then appliqué the inner head (#2) to the head (#1), leaving the top open for stuffing later. Appliqué the mouth (#6) to the bottom circle (#5); then appliqué the bottom circle (#5) to the head (#1). Now stuff the inner head (#2) lightly and close the opening.
4. Place the finished patch face down on a piece of fabric slightly larger than the patch and trace its outline with a dressmaker's carbon pencil. Remove the patch and add a ¼-inch seam allowance to the traced outline.
5. Baste under this ¼-inch seam allowance, baste the lining to the back of the monkey, then neatly whipstitch the edges together. If you want to stuff the monkey patch even more, leave an opening and stuff the lined patch lightly. Be sure to close up the opening. Now the patch is ready to be sewn on whatever you like.

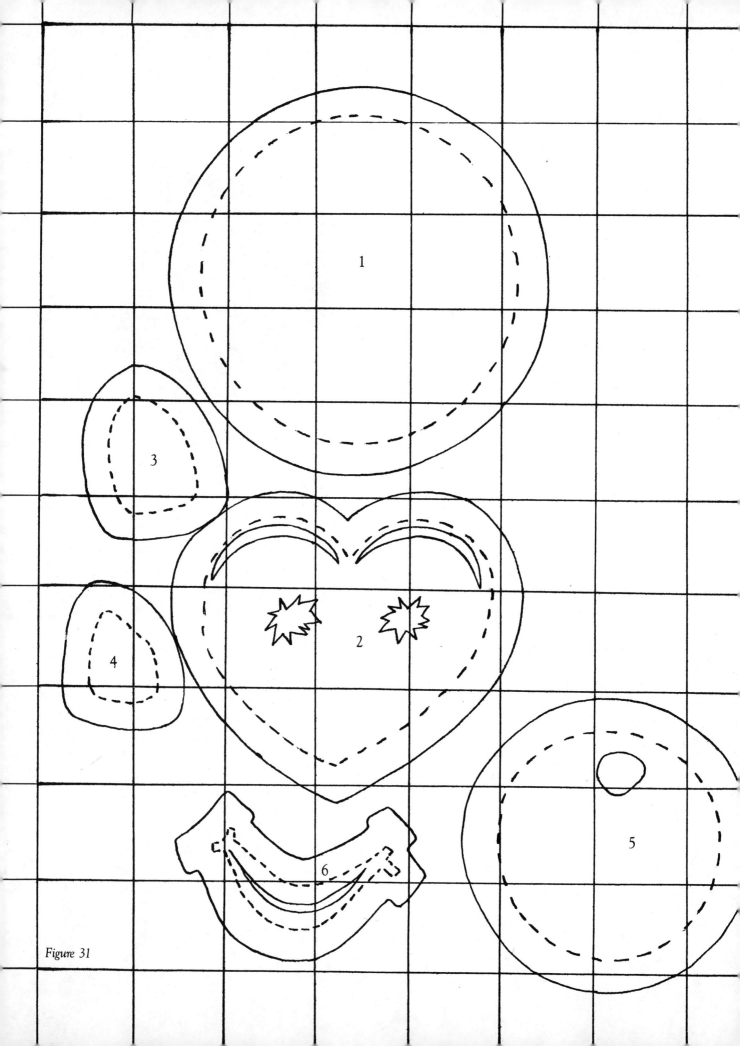

Figure 31

Sun Face

Materials:
Scraps of plain-colored material
Embroidery floss
Small amount of loose polyester stuffing

Directions:
1. Make a template for each of the two parts of the design. You will need to cut one of the face (#2) and eighteen of the sun points (#1). Transfer seam and accent lines to each piece.
2. Before appliquéing the points to the sun face, embroider the mouth and cheeks of the face (#2) in the satin stitch. Use large French knots for the eyes and the chain stitch for the rest of the accent lines on the face.
3. Now appliqué all the sun points (#1) around the edge of the face.

4. Place the finished patch face down on a piece of fabric slightly larger than the patch and trace its outline with a dressmaker's carbon

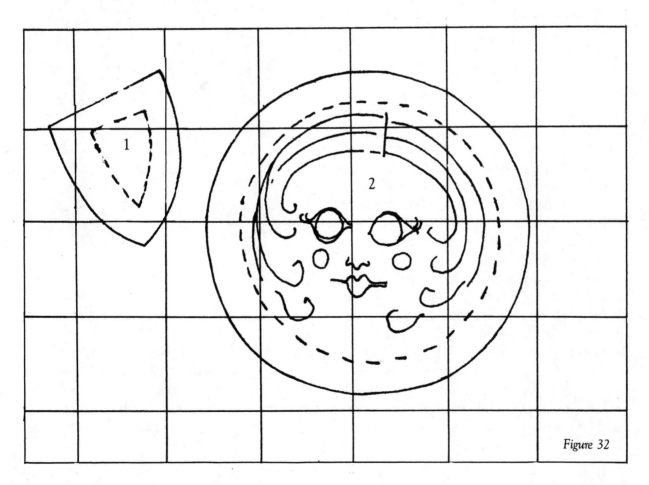

Figure 32

pencil. Remove the patch and add a ¼-inch seam allowance to the traced outline.

5. Baste under this ¼-inch seam allowance, baste the lining to the back of the sun face, and then neatly whipstitch the folded edges together. Leave a small opening and stuff the entire patch lightly but firmly. Close up the opening. Now the patch is ready to be sewn on whatever you like.

Indian Girl

Materials:
Scraps of black and other plain-colored materials
Embroidery floss
Small amount of loose polyester stuffing

Directions:
1. Make a template for each of the four different parts of the design and mark on each how many to cut and from which fabric. You will need to cut two of the hair (#1) from the black fabric, one of the headband (#2), one of the head (#3) and one of the feather (#4). Note on the template for the hair (#1) that you must reverse the template when marking its second outline on the fabric. This way the hair will turn the right way. Transfer seam and accent lines to each piece.
2. Before assembling the patch, embroider the accent lines on the headband (#2) in the chain stitch, and use the satin stitch to fill in the eyes, nose and mouth on the head (#3).
3. Now appliqué the hair (#1) to each side of the head (#3), making sure they meet in the center of the head at the top and extend slightly out to each side. Appliqué the headband (#2) on top of the hair. Finally, appliqué the feather (#4) in place.

4. Place the completed patch face down on a piece of fabric slightly larger than the patch and trace its outline with a dressmaker's carbon pencil. Remove the patch and add a ¼-inch seam allowance to the outline.

5. Baste under this ¼-inch seam allowance; baste the lining to the back of the Indian girl, and then neatly whipstitch the edges together, leaving the bottom of the head open. Stuff the entire patch as fully as you wish and then close up the opening. Now the patch is ready to be sewn on whatever you like.

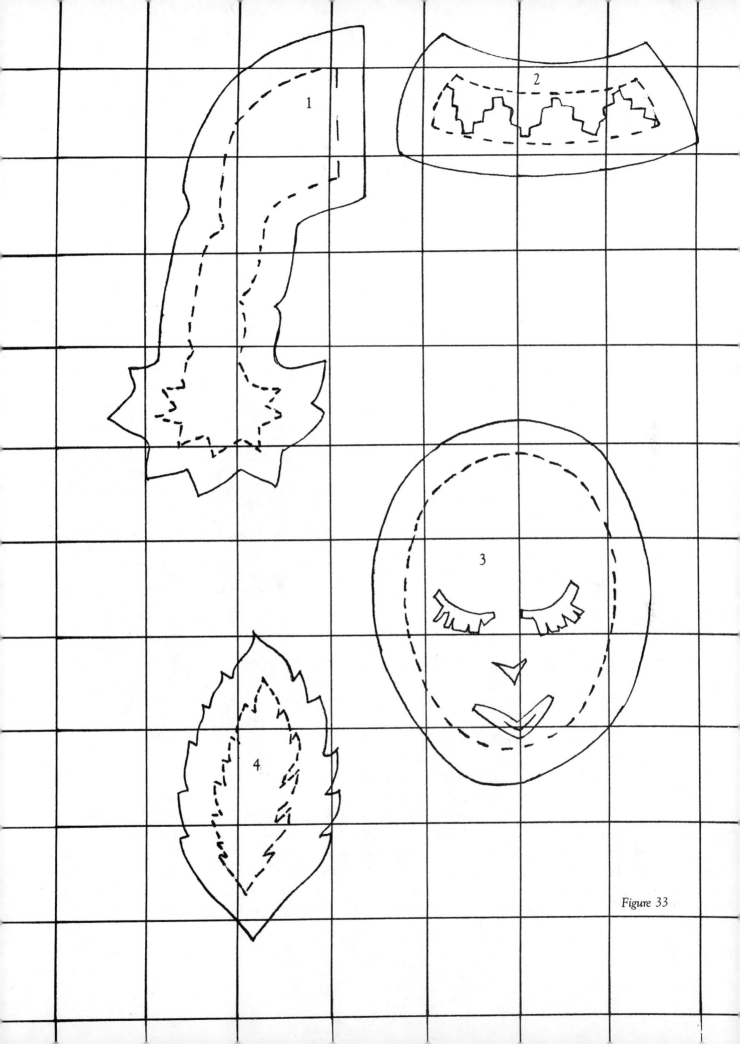

Figure 33

Owl

Materials:
Scraps of plain-colored and print fabric
Embroidery floss
Small amount of loose polyester stuffing

Directions:
1. Make a template for each of the five different parts of the owl and mark on each how many to cut and from which fabric. You will need to cut one of the body of the owl (#1), two of the eye (#2), one of the body bottom (#3), two of the wing (#4) and one of the feet (#5). Note on the template for the wing (#4) that you must reverse the template when marking its second outline on the fabric. This way the two wings will point in the right direction. Transfer seam and accent lines to each piece.
2. Before assembling the owl, embroider the accent marks around the eyes on the body (#1) in the chain stitch and the nose in the satin stitch. On the eye (#2), embroider a large French knot. On the wings (#4), use a chain or stem stitch for the vertical accent line.
3. Appliqué the eyes (#2) in the proper place on the body of the owl (#1), leaving a small opening to stuff them lightly. Be sure to close the opening. Next, appliqué the body bottom (#3) to the lower part of the body of the owl (#1) and leave an opening at the bottom for stuffing. Stuff very fully and close up the opening. Next, appliqué the wings (#4) to the sides of the body of the owl (#1), making sure they extend slightly over each edge, as shown in the illustration. Leave a small opening on the inside part of the wings, but don't stuff them until you have added the lining. Finally, appliqué the feet (#5) in place at the bottom of the owl.
4. Place the finished owl face down on a piece of fabric slightly larger than the patch and

trace its outline with a dressmaker's carbon pencil. Remove the patch and add a ¼-inch seam allowance to the traced outline.

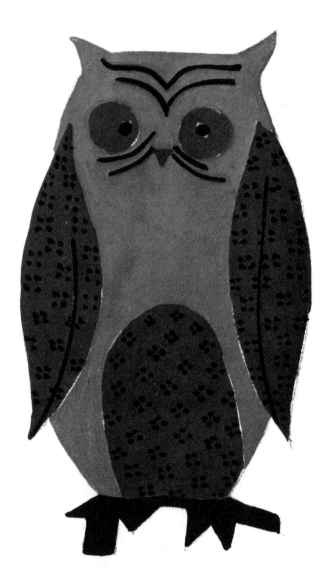

5. Baste under this ¼-inch seam allowance, baste the lining to the back of the owl, and then neatly whipstitch the edges together. Now stuff the wings lightly and close up the opening. The patch is now ready to be sewn on whatever you like.

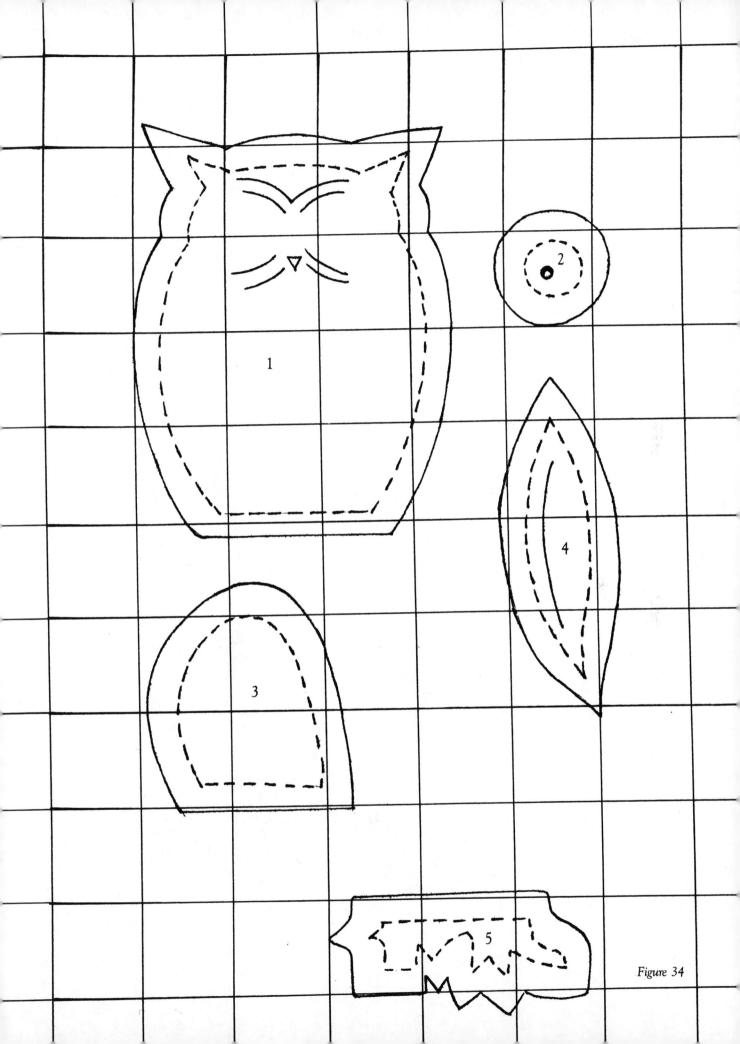

Figure 34

Stuffed Toys

Here are designs for four stuffed toys that should last a long time in the crib or the playpen. They are very easy to make. You just cut two identical shapes, remembering to reverse the template for the second one, whipstitch them together and stuff. What can make these toys special is your choice of fabric and the embroidery work.

Bird

Size:
4½ x 5 inches

Materials:
⅛ yard of plain-colored or print material, 36 inches wide

Embroidery floss
Small amount of loose polyester stuffing

Directions:
1. Make a template for the bird. Cut two, remembering to reverse the template when marking the outline for the second one. Transfer seam and accent lines to each piece.
2. You will do the same embroidery work on both the back and the front of the bird. Work the eye in a French knot. Then do the tail feathers and the beak in the chain stitch.
3. Baste under the seam allowance on both the front and the back. Pin the front and the back together, wrong sides facing, and baste. Whipstitch the folded edges together, using a tiny stitch. Start at the bottom of the beak, go around the head and finish about 1 inch below the beak. Remove the bastings.
4. Stuff the bird very firmly and fully and then whipstitch the opening closed.

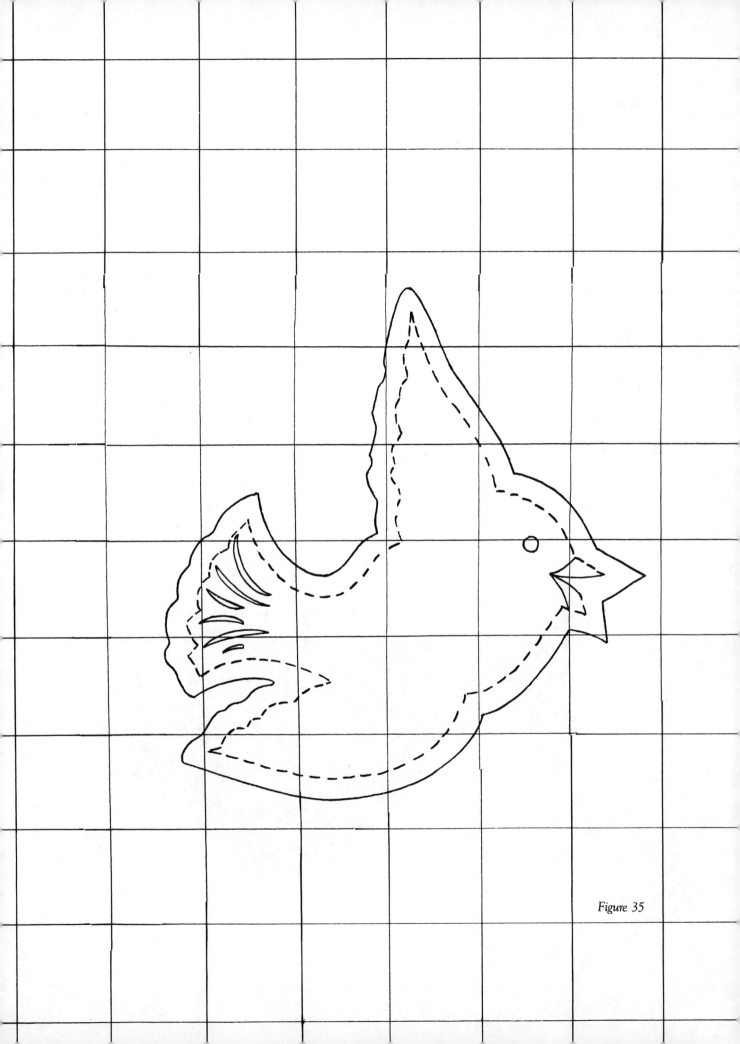

Figure 35

Fish

Size:
5½ x 4¼ inches

Materials:
⅛ yard of plain-colored or print material, 36 inches wide
Embroidery floss
Small amount of loose polyester stuffing

Directions:
1. Make a template for the fish. Cut two, remembering to reverse the template when marking the outline for the second one. Transfer seam and accent lines to each piece.
2. You will do the same embroidery work on both the front and the back. Work the eye in a French knot and the mouth and fin in the chain stitch.
3. Baste under the seam allowance on both the front and the back. Pin the front and the back together, wrong sides facing, and baste. Whipstitch the folded edges together, using a tiny stitch. Start at the fish's back and continue around its tail until you reach about 1 inch from where you began. Remove the bastings.
4. Stuff the fish very firmly and fully; then whipstitch the 1-inch opening closed.

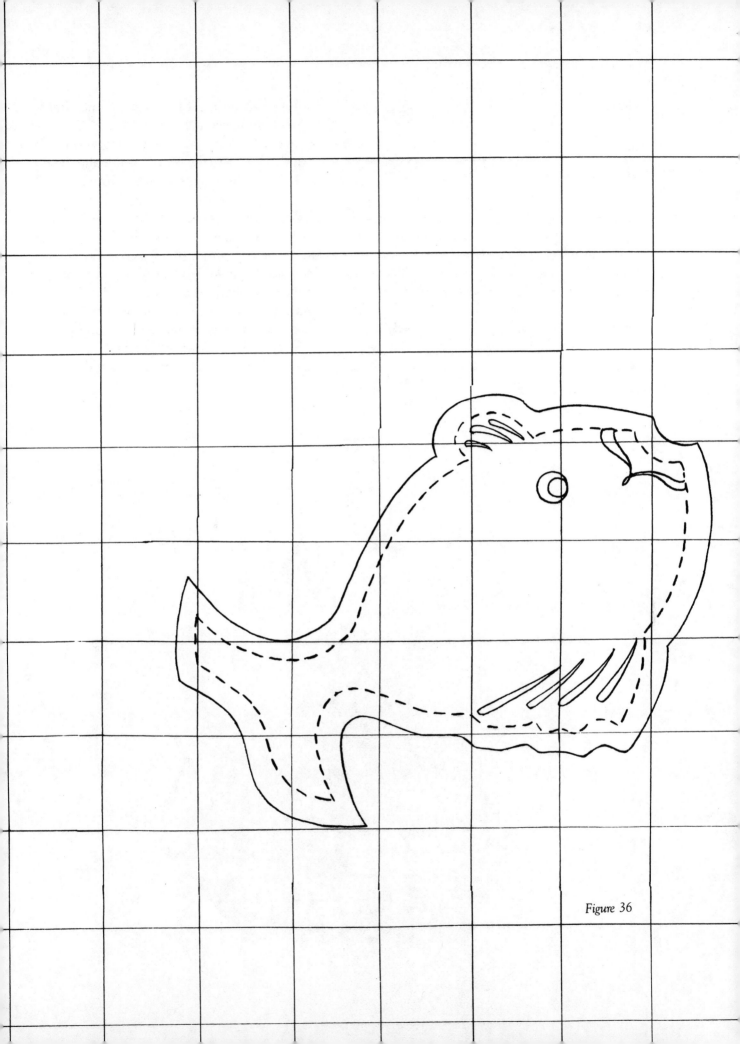

Figure 36

Boat

Size:
4½ x 4½ inches

Materials:
⅛ yard of plain-colored or print material, 36
   inches wide
Embroidery floss
Small amount of loose polyester stuffing

Directions:
1. Make a template for the boat. Cut two,
remembering to reverse the template when
marking the outline for the second one. Transfer seam and accent lines to each piece.
2. You will do the same embroidery work on
both the front and the back. Do the number on
the flag at the top in the satin stitch and the sail
lines in the chain stitch.
3. Baste under the seam allowance on both
the front and the back. Pin the front and the
back together, wrong sides facing, and baste.
Whipstitch the folded edges together, using a
tiny stitch. Start at one side of the sail and
continue around the boat until within 1 inch of
where you started. Remove the bastings.
4. Stuff the boat very firmly and fully and then
whipstitch the 1-inch opening closed.

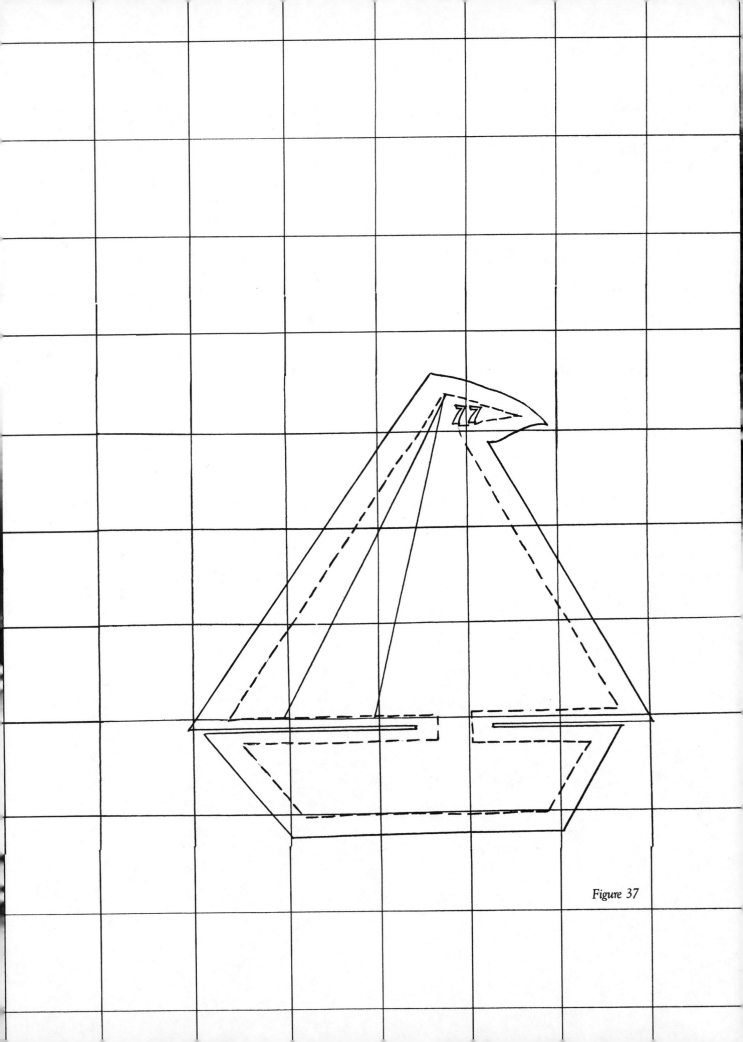

Figure 37

Train

Size:
4½ x 4½ inches

Materials:
⅛ yard of plain-colored or print material, 36 inches wide
Embroidery floss
Small amount of loose polyester stuffing

Directions:
1. Make a template for the train. Cut two, remembering to reverse the template when marking the outline for the second one. Transfer seam and accent lines to each piece.
2. You will do the same embroidery work on both the front and the back. Do the windows in the satin stitch and both the top of the smokestack and the front loader in the chain stitch.
3. Baste under the seam allowance on both the front and the back. Pin the front and the back together, wrong sides facing, and baste. Whipstitch the folded edges together, using a tiny stitch. Start at the bottom of the train and continue around the train until within 1 inch of where you started. Remove the bastings.
4. Stuff the train very firmly and fully and then whipstitch the 1-inch opening closed.

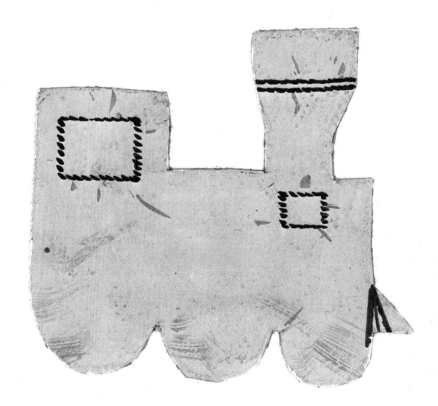

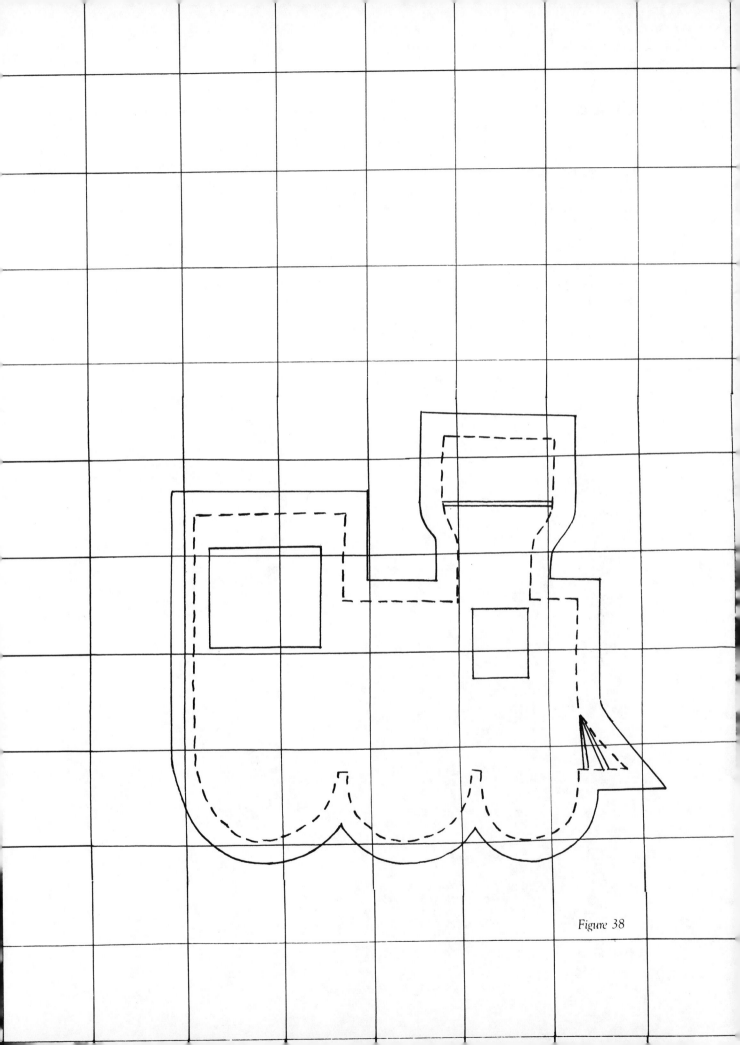

Figure 38

Children's Sleeping Bags

Here are two designs to put on kids' sleeping bags. The bags themselves are remarkably easy to make, and children find them a lot of fun to sleep in. These are not outdoor sleeping bags; they are really not warm enough for a cold night. But they are fine for indoors anytime, and I would not hesitate to use them outside if the night promised to be warm and dry. The bags are constructed in two parts, each having three layers quilted for warmth and comfort. The top part has the design on it and the bottom is plain. They are joined at the long sides and the bottom with buttons, a strip of Velcro, or a long separating zipper—whichever takes your fancy. This way it is easy to separate the two parts to wash them.

Size:
31 x 54 inches

Appears in color on page 34

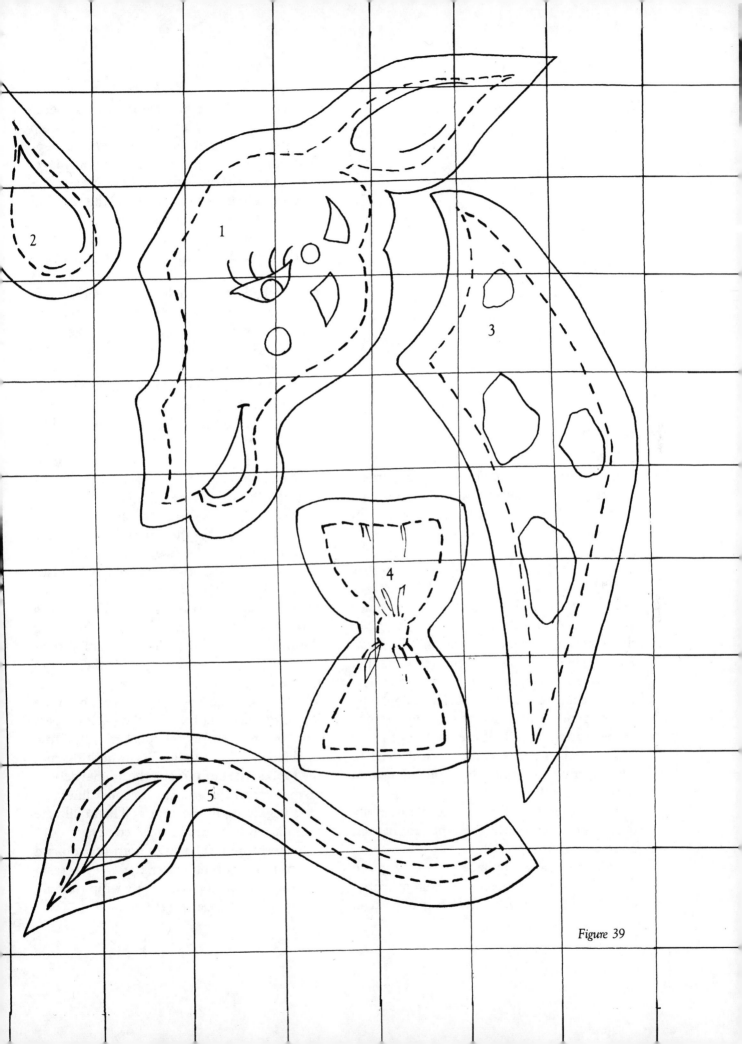

Figure 39

Materials:

3½ yards of plain-colored material, 36 inches wide for top and back of bag

3½ yards of plain-colored lining material, 36 inches wide (This could be the same material you use for the top and the back).

½ yard of yellow material, 36 inches wide, for the animal shapes

Embroidery floss

Large roll of batting

Small amount of loose polyester stuffing

Velcro, buttons or a long separating zipper for use on the sides and bottom of the sleeping bag.

Directions:

1. Make templates for each of the five different parts of the design you choose. Enlarge them by using 2-inch squares, rather than 1-inch squares as shown. You will cut one of each. Transfer all accent and seam lines to each piece.

2. Cut the top and the back of the sleeping bag to the required size—31½ x 54½ inches—making sure to mark a ¼-inch seam allowance all around. Also, cut two of the lining fabric to the same size as that of the top and the back. Finally, cut two pieces of batting the same size.

3. There is a certain amount of embroidery work you must do before you begin to appliqué. For the giraffe, embroider the spots on the neck in the satin stitch and the eyes in the outline or chain stitch. For the lion, you will need to embroider all the accent lines on the face in the chain stitch.

4. Study the illustration on page 94 carefully to see where to place the different parts of each animal.

5. For the giraffe, appliqué the ear in place first, leaving a small opening to stuff it lightly. Close up the opening. Next, appliqué the head

in place and leave an opening at the neck. Stuff the head fairly firmly, but do not close up the opening. Slip the neck into the head opening and stuff both. Close up the openings. Next comes the tail. Stuff this lightly and close up the opening. Finally, appliqué the bow and stuff it lightly. Close up the opening. Add the final embroidery work by outlining the knobs on the top of the giraffe's head with the chain stitch.

6. For the lion, you will appliqué the centers of the two paws in place before sewing them to the top. When this is done, appliqué the lion's head in place and leave an opening to stuff quite firmly. Close up the opening. Now appliqué the two paws in place and stuff them only lightly. Close up the opening.

7. Mark the quilting lines on the top first. Use an outline pattern around the animals, and fill the rest of the open space with straight diagonal lines. For the back, simply use diagonal lines in a diamond pattern.

8. Now you are ready to assemble the parts of the sleeping bag. For the top half, place a piece of batting on a flat surface. On top of it place the completed top, right side up. Now place the lining face down on the top. Pin and then baste around the two long sides and the bottom of the three layers and sew them together along the marked seam lines. Turn the lining right side out. Do exactly the same for the back of the sleeping bag.

9. Now baste the layers together for both the top of the sleeping bag and the back so there will be no accidental puckering of the thicknesses as you quilt. Begin quilting. On the top, do the outlining of the animal designs first and then the straight diagonal lines, always beginning in the center. Then quilt the back, again beginning in the center.

10. Finish the raw edges of both the top and the back by turning under the ¼-inch seam allowance at the top and neatly whipstitching the two folded edges together.

Figure 40

11. Join the two long edges and the bottom of the top and back by attaching buttons, a strip of Velcro, or a long separating zipper.

Gingham Flower Quilt

This attractive crib quilt makes an ideal baby gift. If the child is a boy, use blue-checked gingham; if she turns out to be a girl, use pink. Embroider as much or as little information as you like on the flower centers. If you leave several blank, you can add additional information when a newer baby appears on the scene. I particularly like a ruffled edging on this quilt and suggest you try it.

Size:
45 x 60 inches

Materials:
4½ yards of checked gingham material, 48 inches wide, for the top, backing and ruffled edging
¼ yard of green material, 36 inches wide, for the leaves and stems
¼ yard of white material, 36 inches wide, for the flower centers
½ yard of yellow material, 36 inches wide, for the petals
Embroidery floss
Small roll of batting
Small amount of loose polyester stuffing

Directions:
1. Make templates for each of the four different parts of the design. Mark on each how many pieces to cut and from what color fabric. You will need to cut eight flower centers (#1) from the white fabric, eight stems (#3) and sixteen leaves (#4) from the green fabric and fifty-six petals (#2) from the yellow fabric. Transfer seam lines to each piece.
2. Cut out the top of the quilt to the correct size—45½ x 60½ inches—and mark a ¼-inch seam allowance all around.
3. Before appliquéing the flower centers to the top of the quilt, embroider the name of the baby, date of birth and weight in three flower centers. Use a chain or outline stitch for this. If another baby comes along, you can always remove the blank centers, embroider them appropriately and then return them to the quilt.
4. Study carefully the illustration opposite and note how the flowers are positioned. Be sure to space them evenly so they will look as if they are growing in a garden.
5. Appliqué the flowers in place, beginning in each case with the centers (#1). Leave openings to stuff the centers very fully and firmly. Close up the openings. Next, appliqué the stems (#3). Leave an opening at each base and stuff the stems lightly. Close up the openings. Next appliqué the flower petals (#2) around the center. These you should stuff only lightly. Finally, appliqué the leaves and stuff them very fully. Close up the openings.
6. Mark the quilting lines. Use an outline design around all parts of the flower and stems and fill in the open spaces either with straight diagonal lines or lines following the checks of the gingham.
7. Cut the batting and backing to the proper size and baste the top, batting and backing together securely.
8. Begin quilting by outlining the flowers first and then, starting in the center of the quilt top, the straight lines.
9. Finish the raw edges by attaching a ruffled edging. Complete directions for this are given on page 26.

Appears in color on page 34

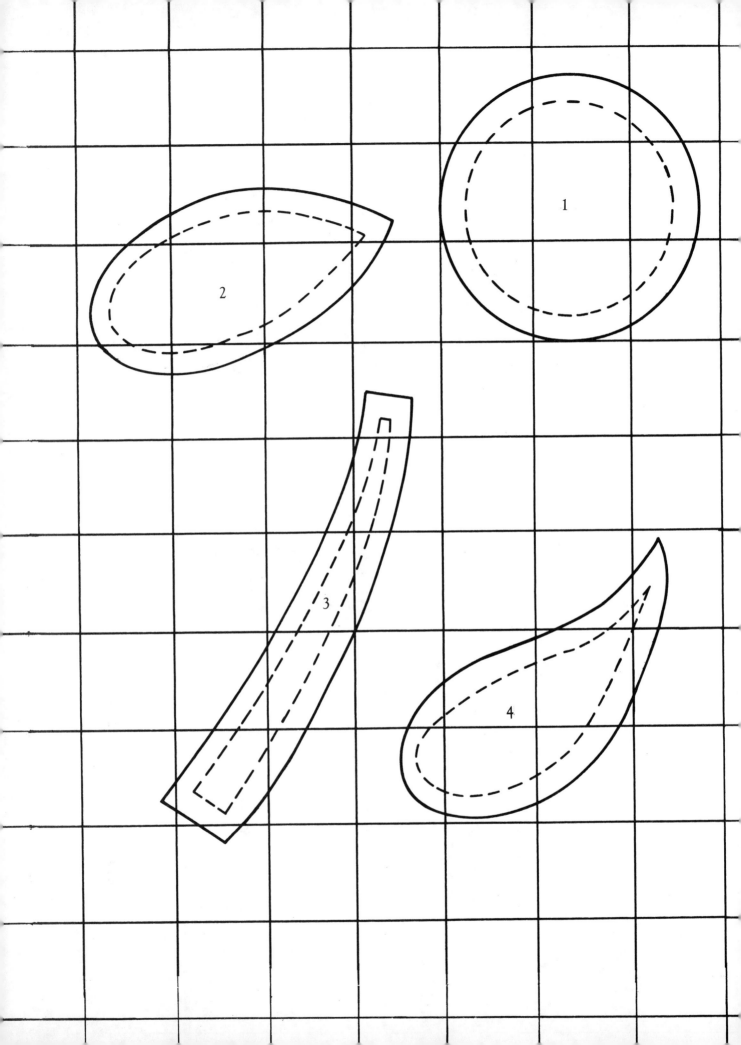

Circus Quilt

The design on this charming child's quilt should look familiar. Some of the figures are the same ones I used on the tops of the sleeping bags. I included some of the same designs again so you will get a feel for how designs can be combined or used to advantage in different settings. You will find the patterns for the giraffe and the lion's head on pages 95 to 97. I think the best binding for this quilt is one made out of purchased bias binding. Pick one of the bright colors you have used for one of the animals or part of the clown.

Size:
69 x 82 inches

Materials:
5 yards of white or off-white background material, 36 inches wide, for the top
5 yards of white or off-white material, 36 inches wide, for the backing
½ yard of material, 36 inches wide, for each different figure, depending on your choice of color and fabric
Embroidery floss
Small roll of batting
Small amount of loose polyester stuffing
Bias binding (optional)

Directions:
1. Make a template for each of the different parts of each figure. Enlarge all of them by using 2-inch squares, rather than the 1-inch squares as shown. Mark on each how many to cut and from which fabric. For the elephant, you will need to cut one head and two ears, remembering to reverse the template when marking the second ear. For the giraffe, you will need to cut one head and one ear. For the lion, you will need to cut one head. For the clown, you will need to cut one of each of the parts. Transfer all accent lines and seam lines to each of the pieces.

2. Cut and piece both the top and the backing to the proper size—69½ x 82½ inches. Mark a ¼-inch seam allowance all around.

3. Here is the embroidery work you should do before you begin to appliqué: On the giraffe, embroider the spots in the satin stitch and the other accent lines in the chain stitch. Use the chain stitch for all the accent lines on the lion's head and the elephant. However, do not embroider the tusks on the elephant until after you appliqué. On the clown, use French knots for his eyes and use the satin stitch for his hatband, nose, hair, the buttons on his trousers and the toes of his open shoe. Use the chain stitch for the rest of the accent lines.

4. Study the illustration on page 102 to see where to place each of the figures. Begin with the giraffe. Appliqué his ear and stuff lightly. Close up the opening. Now appliqué his head and leave an opening to stuff it fully. Close up the opening. Embroider the knobs at the top of his head in the satin stitch.

5. Appliqué the lion's head in place. Leave an opening and stuff it very fully. Close up the opening.

6. Appliqué the elephant's head. Leave an opening at both sides to slip in the ears. Appliqué the ears in place on each side of the head. Stuff them lightly and close up the opening. Now stuff the elephant's head quite fully and close up the opening. Embroider the tusks in place, using the satin stitch.

7. Appliqué the clown's head and leave an opening at the bottom to stuff later. Appliqué the hat next, stuff it fully and close up the opening. Now stuff the head lightly and close up the opening. Appliqué the two sides of the coat and the shirt front, checking the illustration for placement. Leave the bottom of each open so you can slip the top of the pants in place. However, you will not stuff the coat. Appliqué the pants, leaving the bottoms open for the shoes. Now finish appliquéing the coat and the shirt front. Appliqué the shoes in place and then slightly stuff the pants and close up

Appears in color on page 35

the opening. Appliqué the hands in place. Finally, appliqué the bow tie at the top of the coat and shirt front. Stuff it lightly if you wish and close up the opening. Appliqué the umbrella. Finally, embroider the umbrella handle in the chain stitch.

8. Mark your quilting lines. I would suggest outlining each of the figures and then using diagonal lines for the rest of the open spaces.

9. Cut the batting to the proper size and baste the top, batting and backing together securely. Begin quilting through the center of the top and continue quilting until all quilting lines have been completely stitched.

10. Finish the raw edges by adding bias binding, if you wish.

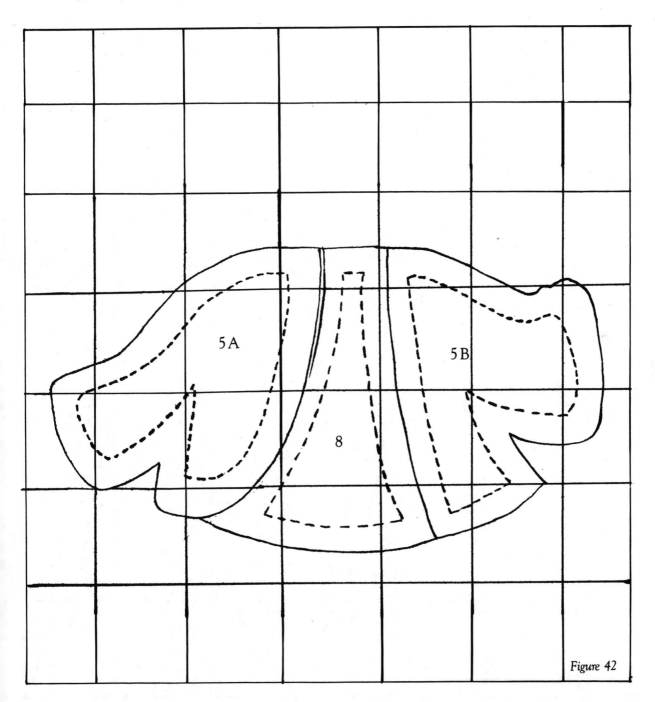

Figure 42

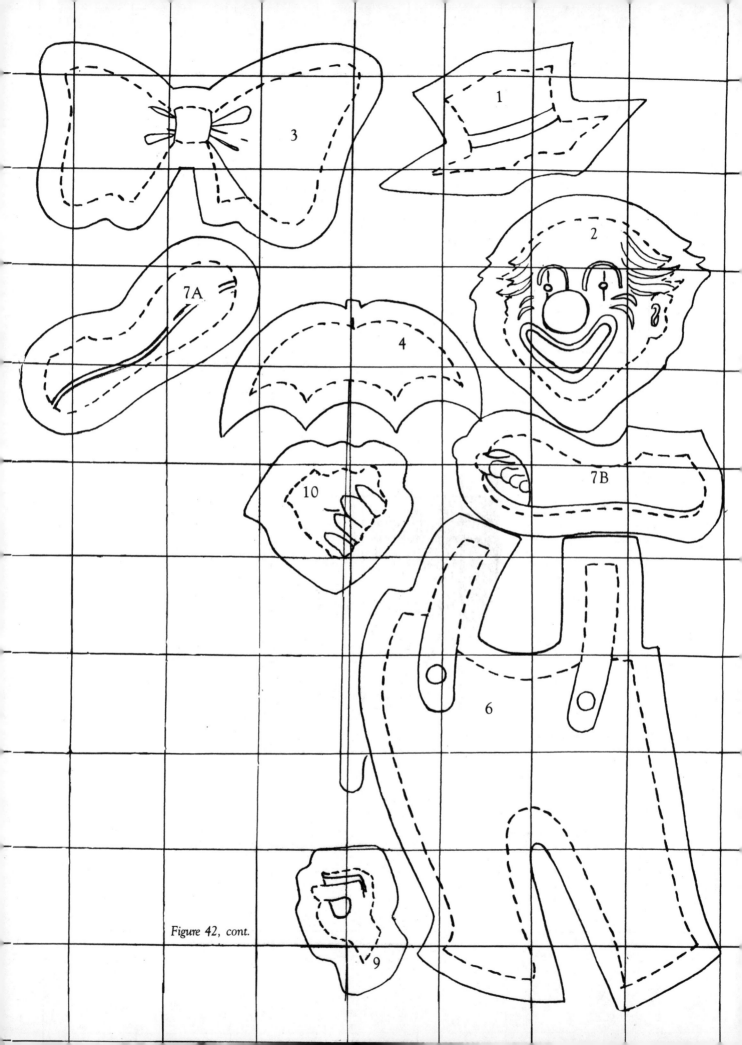

Figure 42, cont.

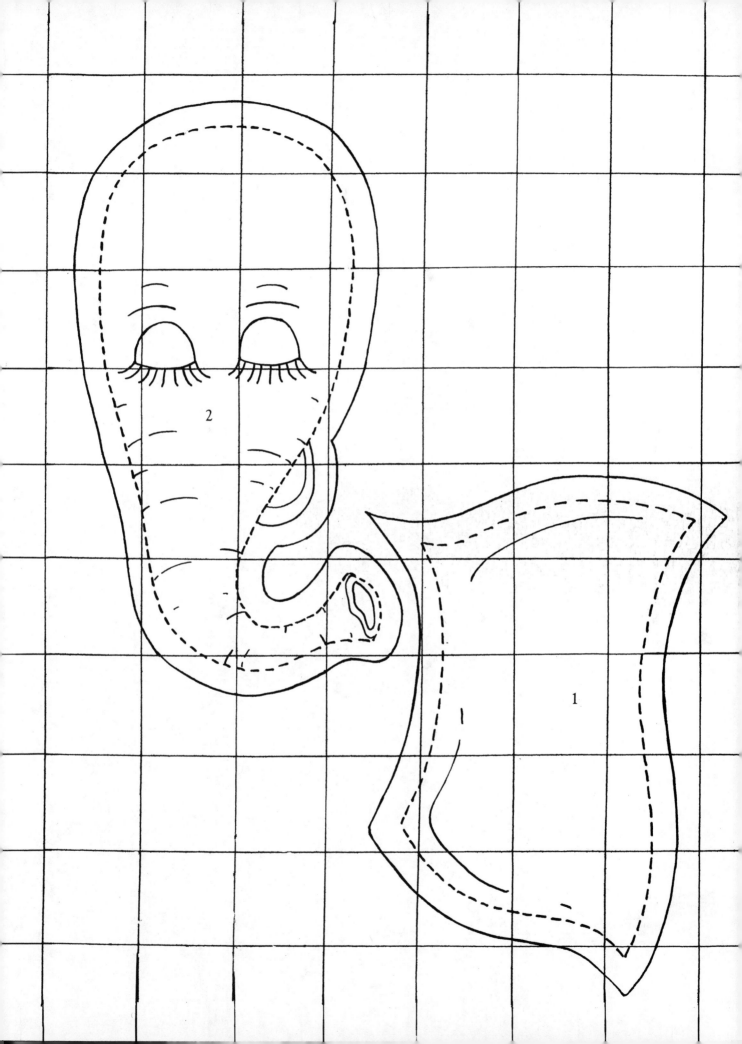

Appears in color on page 36

Flying Mother Goose Quilt

This is one of my favorite designs for a child's quilt. It is quite a complicated one, with its thirteen different design parts and its many embroidery accents, but I think it's well worth the effort. The top is made out of blocks, so if you like you can leave alternating blocks empty, which would cut your work load considerably and still give you a fine quilt. No two flying Mother Goose designs ever come out looking the same because of the wide variety of fabrics you can choose for the scarf, coat, skirt, etc. I've chosen colors that are rather muted, but brighter colors are just as effective. I would finish the edges of this quilt either by self-binding or by adding bias binding.

Size:
45 x 54 inches
30 blocks—5 across and 6 down

Materials:
4 yards of white or off-white material, 48 inches wide, for the top and backing
½ yard of material, 45 inches wide, for each different shape of the design
Embroidery floss
Small amount of yarn
Small roll of batting
Small amount of loose polyester stuffing
Bias binding (optional)

Directions:
1. Make a template for each of the thirteen different parts of the design. The number of pieces to cut depends on the number of squares on which you wish to place the design. If you decide to use it on every square, you will need to cut thirty pieces from each template. If you choose to leave some squares plain, count the number with designs on them; this will be the number of pieces to cut from each template.

Mark on each template how many pieces to cut and from which fabric.
2. Cut out all the pieces of the design and transfer seam and accent lines to each piece. Also, cut out thirty 9½-inch squares from the white or off-white fabric. Mark on each the ¼-inch seam allowance.
3. There is some embroidery work you must do before you begin to appliqué. On the hat (#1), work the hatband and buckle in the satin stitch. On the head (#2), both the cheek and the small circles in the eyes can be done in the satin stitch. Outline the eyes, the mouth and the hair in the chain stitch. On the head of the goose (#7), use the satin stitch for the shoe and two French knots for the buttons. Both the rein and the eye of the goose should also be done in the satin stitch. On the wing (#8), do the accent marks very close together in the chain stitch. Attach the fringe to the ends of the scarf (#6) in the following way: Make several loops of doubled yarn, tie a large knot at the end of each and then cut the loops. Whipstitch the knots, evenly spaced, to the ends of the scarf.
4. Check the illustration opposite to see how to position the various pieces of the design. Appliqué the tail of the goose (#9) first, leaving part of the top open. Stuff it lightly and close up the opening. Next, appliqué the foot (#10) below the tail. Now appliqué the wing (#8) and stuff it lightly. Close up the opening. Appliqué the skirt (#5); do not stuff it. The head of the goose (#7) comes next. Leave an opening at the top of the head and stuff it lightly. Close up the opening. Now appliqué the beak (#11) in front of the head. Appliqué the blouse (#3) and stuff it lightly. Close up the opening. Again checking the illustration, appliqué first the right hand (#12) and then the left hand (#13). Now appliqué the head (#2) in place, tilting it slightly. Leave the top open and stuff it lightly. Close up the opening. Appliqué the collar (#4) in place; do not stuff. Appliqué the scarf (#6); do not stuff. Finally,

Figure 43

appliqué the hat (#1) in place, making sure it is at the proper angle. Slightly stuff the hat and close up the opening.

5. Do the final embroidery work. On the blouse (#3), work the arm in the satin stitch. On the left hand (#13), finish the rein and the fingers of the hand in the satin stitch.

6. Finish each block completely before you begin another.

7. Join all the blocks for the top together. Lay them out in their proper order on a flat surface. You should have five blocks across and six down. If you have left some squares empty, put them in the appropriate place. Piece the blocks together, beginning in the center of the top. Baste and then sew on the seam lines, making sure corners meet exactly. Remove bastings and press seams open.

8. When the top is completed, mark quilting lines on it. I would suggest using an outline pattern around the various parts of the design and diagonal lines for the open spaces. If you have included some plain blocks, you might use your design templates as a guide and trace them in the plain squares. Quilt them in a contrasting color of thread so the design will show up, or you could use diagonal quilting lines in the plain squares.

9. Cut the backing and the batting to the proper size—45½ x 54½ inches—and then baste the top, batting and backing together. Begin quilting through the center of the top and continue quilting until all quilting lines have been completely stitched.

10. Finish the raw edges either by adding bias binding or with self-binding.

5. Designs for the Home

Card-Table Cover

If you are an inveterate cardplayer, as I am, this interesting card-table cover should appeal to you. If the table on which you play cards is a different size, use its dimensions rather than the ones I have given, and space the cards appropriately. I have suggested several different fabrics for the cover itself—cotton, linen and velvet. Cotton and linen can be quilted and washed; but velvet should not be quilted and, of course, can't be washed.

Size:
36 x 36 inches

Materials:
1½ yards of cotton, linen or velvet, 45 inches wide, for the top and side drop
1 yard of lining material, 45 inches wide, for the backing
½ yard of the same material as for top and side drop for the cards
¼ yard of red material, 36 inches wide, for the hearts and diamonds
¼ yard of black material, 36 inches wide, for the spades and clubs
Embroidery floss
Bias binding
Small roll of batting
Small amount of loose polyester stuffing

Directions:
1. Make templates for each different part of the design. Mark on each the number to cut. You will need to cut one each of the heart, diamond, club and spade figures, one of the large heart for the center and twelve of the card shape. (All the numbers and suits that appear on the cards are embroidered.) Transfer seam lines to each piece.
2. For the cover itself cut a square 36½ x 36½ inches from the top cover fabric. Next, cut out a 3-inch drop from the same fabric. Make it long enough to fit around the entire edge of the cover. Be sure to allow ¼-inch seam allowance along one long side to attach it to the cover and ¼-inch along the other side for a narrow hem. Sew the drop to the cover square. Turn up the hem on the drop. Some people like to put ties at all four corners to make the cover fit the table more tightly. Use purchased bias binding for this. You might also attach this same bias binding on the hem of the drop if you like.
3. Embroider all the numbers on the cards before you appliqué them. Use the chain or outline stitch for this. When you embroider the suits on the cards, do it with the satin stitch in the appropriate color of floss.
4. Now appliqué the cards to the cover. Check the illustration opposite for correct spacing. Use either machine or hand sewing. If you choose to stitch by machine, I suggest

using a zigzag stitch, since it gives more accent. Leave a small opening on the cards to stuff them lightly. Be sure the stuffing is very evenly distributed before closing up the opening. Next, appliqué the suits in the four corners. Stuff these *lightly* as well and close up the opening. Finally, appliqué the large heart in the center of the cloth. Do not stuff this.

5. Mark the quilting lines on the cover. Do not mark quilting lines on the drop. I suggest using an outline stitch around the four suit figures in the corners and around the cards. For the rest of the open space, mark square or diagonal straight lines.

6. Cut batting and lining fabric to the size of the cover, not including the drop, being sure to add ¼-inch seam allowance all around. Baste the three layers together securely.

7. Begin quilting. Do all your outline quilting before you begin to quilt the straight lines. Start in the middle of the cover and work toward the sides. Continue quilting until all lines have been completely stitched.

8. Turn the cover and fold under the ¼-inch seam allowance on all sides of the backing. Trim the batting, if necessary. Whipstitch the folded edge of the backing to the seam allowance of the drop.

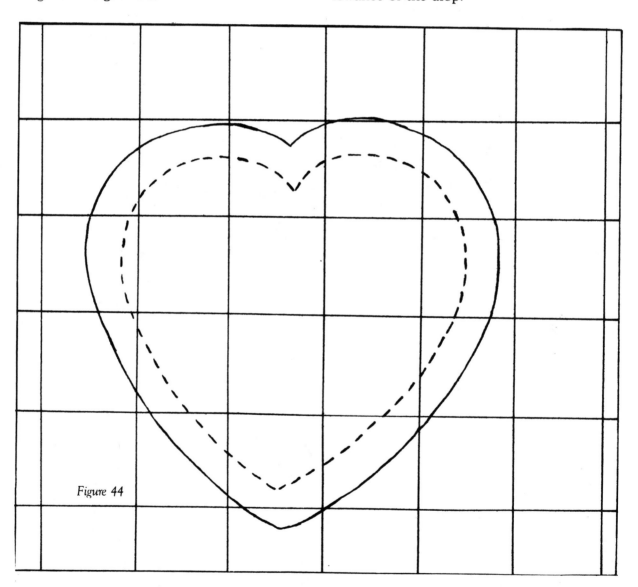

Figure 44

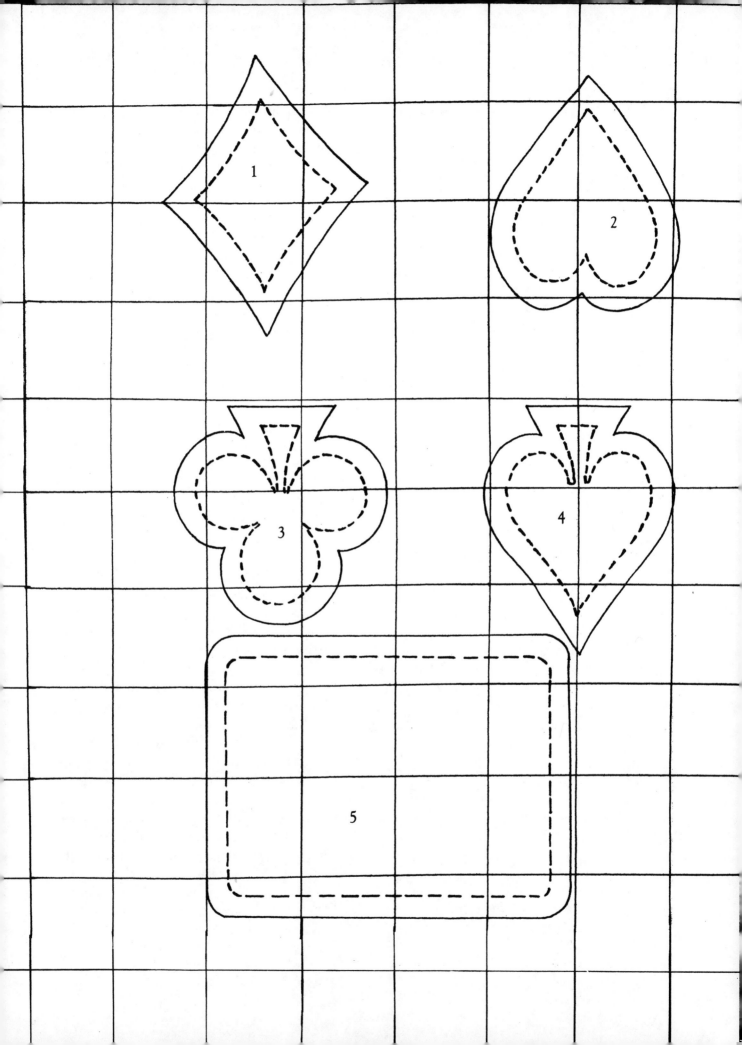

Wall Hangings

Fabric wall hangings have become enormously popular, and I think for good reason. The texture of the materials used and the three-dimensional quality produced by stuffing and quilting give them a look totally different from ordinary pictures. Here are three of my designs for you to choose from. I have suggested that you enlarge the designs, but they are equally attractive in a smaller size and framed so they look more like a picture than a hanging. The two flower designs are shown with a contrasting border, which is attached in the same way you add a border to a quilt. If you make the hangings the size I've suggested, you will probably want to use dowels inserted into fabric loops at the top and bottom to hold them straight. These sticks are available at most hardware stores.

Daffodil

Size:
16 x 24 inches

Materials:
½ yard of pale blue material, 36 inches wide, for the top background
½ yard of backing material, 36 inches wide
⅛ yard of green material, 36 inches wide, for the stems and leaves
⅛ yard of yellow material, 36 inches wide, for the flower and petals
Embroidery floss
Small roll of batting
Small amount of loose polyester stuffing
Bias binding (optional)
Dowels (optional)

Directions:
1. Make templates for each of the seven parts of the design. Enlarge them by using 2-inch squares, rather than the 1-inch squares given in Figure 45. Mark on each how many to cut and from which fabric. You will need to cut one of the flower (#1), one of the small leaf (#2), one of the small petal (#3), two of the large petal (#4), one of the leaf (#5), one of the stem (#6) and one of the bending leaf (#7). Transfer seam and accent lines to each piece.
2. You will also need to cut three rectangles, each measuring 16½ x 24½ inches—one rectangle from the top background material, one from the batting and one from the lining material. Mark a ¼-inch seam allowance on each rectangle.
3. Before beginning to appliqué, embroider the three stamens in the flower (#1) in the satin stitch and the other accent lines in the chain stitch. Embroider all other accent lines on the petals and leaves in the chain stitch.
4. Study the illustration opposite to see how to position the different parts of the design. Appliqué the flower (#1) first, leaving the sides open until you have added the petals. Appliqué the small petal (#3) and the large petals (#4) on the sides of the flower, leaving a small opening in each for stuffing. Stuff each of them lightly and close up the opening. Now close up one side of the flower (#1). Stuff the flower quite fully from the other side and close up the opening. Appliqué the stem (#6), making sure it fits right under the flower. Leave an opening at the bottom of the stem for stuffing. Now, using the satin stitch, embroider the small accent leaves under the bottom of the flower. Check the illustration for the pattern of these accent leaves. Now stuff the stem, using a long, thin knitting needle. Stuff lightly and close up the opening. Appliqué the bending leaf (#7) toward the bottom of the stem, leaving one side open. Stuff the leaf lightly and close up the opening. Finally, appliqué the small leaf (#2) and leaf #5 on the other side of the stem. Leave an opening in both and stuff them lightly. Close up the opening.

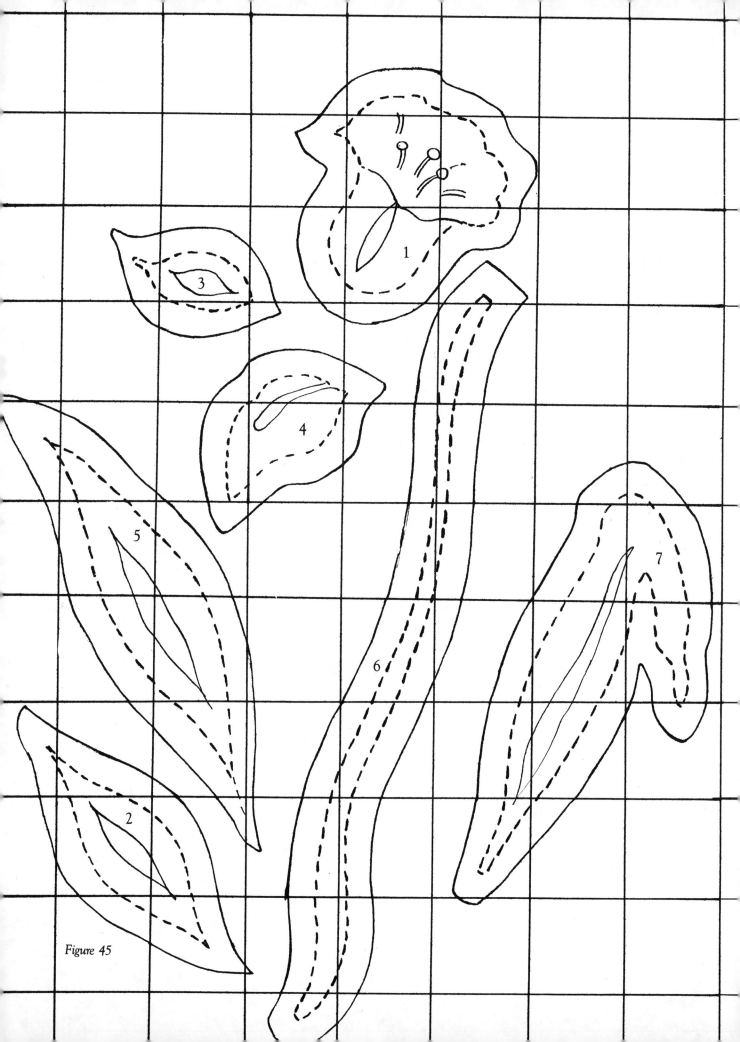

Figure 45

5. Mark the quilting lines. Outline all parts of the flower, and if you wish to do more quilting, I suggest using parallel horizontal lines in the open spaces.

6. Baste together the top, batting and lining material.

7. Quilt on the marked lines until all have been completely stitched.

8. To finish the edges, either whipstitch them neatly together or add a contrasting border. If you intend to frame the design, you need only trim away the excess batting before inserting it in the frame.

Pansy

Size:
20 x 28 inches

Materials:
¾ yard of pale pink material, 36 inches wide, for the top background
¾ yard of backing material, 36 inches wide
⅛ yard of green material, 36 inches wide, for the leaves and stems
¼ yard of green material, 36 inches wide, for the leaves and stems
¼ yard of purple material, 36 inches wide, for the flower
¼ yard of blue material, 36 inches wide, for the flower
¼ yard of pink material, 36 inches wide, for the flower
Embroidery floss
Small roll of batting
Small amount of loose polyester stuffing
Bias binding (optional)
Dowels (optional)

Directions:
1. Make a template for each of the eight parts of the design. Enlarge them by using 2-inch squares, rather than the 1-inch squares given in Figure 46. Mark on each how many to cut and from which fabric. Two of the design parts—the flower (#1) and the center of the flower (#2)—will be cut with pinking shears and no seam allowance, since they will not be appliquéd in the usual way, but rather tacked underneath close to the pinked edges. You will need to cut two of the flower (#1), two of the flower center (#2), one of the stem (#3), six of the petal (#4), two of leaf #5-A, one of leaf #5-B and one of the short stem (#6). Transfer seam and accent lines to each piece.

2. You will also need to cut three rectangles, each measuring 20½ x 28½ inches—one rectangle from the top background material, one from the batting and one from the lining material. Mark a ¼-inch seam allowance on each rectangle.

3. Before beginning to appliqué, embroider the accent lines on the leaves in the chain stitch.

4. Study the illustration on page 118 carefully. You will see that the petals (#4) are layered; three are used for each flower. Arrange them so that one petal in each flower shows completely and the other two are shown only in part. Appliqué the petals in place on the top background material. Next, tack the center of the flower (#2) to the flower (#1), making sure to center it. Now embroider the French knot in the center of #2, as shown in the illustration. Tack the flower (#1) on top of the petals, catching it in the center under the French knot and also catching it underneath the pinked edges. Don't sew them down flat, since the edges should be able to move freely. Now appliqué the long stem (#3) in place, leaving the bottom open for stuffing. Using a long, thin knitting needle, stuff it lightly and close up the opening. Appliqué the short stem (#6) next, leaving an opening, and stuff it lightly. Close up the opening. Now appliqué the leaves (#5-A and #5-B) in place, leaving the lower

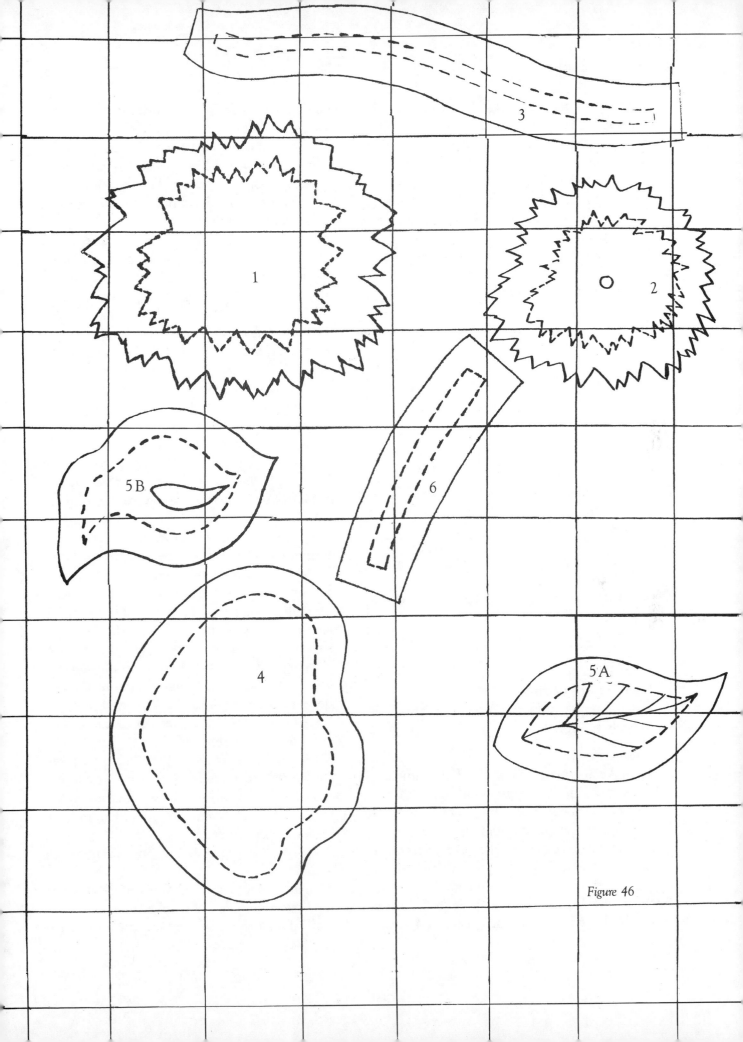

Figure 46

edges open. Stuff them lightly and close up the opening. Check the illustration to see where the lines go that indicate the petal divisions on the flower. Embroider these in the chain stitch.

5. Mark the quilting lines. Outline all parts of the design, and if you wish to do more quilting, I suggest using parallel horizontal lines in the open spaces.

6. Baste together the top, batting and lining material.

7. Quilt on the marked lines until all have been completely stitched.

8. To finish the edges, either whipstitch them together neatly or add a contrasting border. If you intend to frame the design, you need only trim away the excess batting before inserting it in the frame.

House

Size:

8 x 13 inches

Materials:

¼ yard of plain-colored material, 36 inches wide, for the house

⅛ yard of plain-colored material, 36 inches wide, for the roof and grass

Large scraps of print and plaid material for the rest of the design

Embroidery floss

Small roll of batting

Small amount of loose polyester stuffing

Dowels (optional)

Directions:

1. Make templates for each of the nine different parts of the design. Mark on each how many to cut and from which fabric. You will need to cut one of the roof (#1), one of the house (#2), six of the curtain (#3) (remembering to reverse the template when you cut the last three), one of the door (#4), one of the grass (#5), three of the stone (#6), one of the bush (#7), one of the treetop (#8) and

one of the trunk (#9). Transfer the seam lines to each piece.

2. You will not cut the backing or batting now. Cut it after the top has been completely assembled, so that you can use the top as a pattern.

3. Embroider the doorknob on the door (#4) in a French knot.

4. Study the illustration opposite to see how the different parts of the design are placed. First, appliqué the roof (#1) to the top edge of the house (#2). Next, appliqué the curtains (#3) in place on the house. Appliqué the door (#4) in the center of the lower part of the house. Appliqué the grass (#5) to the lower edge of the house. Appliqué the tree trunk (#9) in place. Leave an opening at the bottom to stuff it lightly. Close up the opening. Appliqué the treetop (#8) at the top of the trunk. Leave a small opening at the side of treetop near the center of the house for stuffing later. Appliqué the bush (#7) in place. Leave a small opening at the side toward the center of the house for stuffing later. Finally, appliqué the stones (#6) on the grass, leaving an opening, and stuff lightly. Close up the openings.

5. Mark quilting lines on the top of the assembled house. Study the illustration for ideas. You might use parallel horizontal lines on the roof to suggest shingles and on the house to suggest clapboards. On the grass, use the pattern of curved lines shown in the illustration. You could also mark straight lines on the windows to suggest panes. Do not mark quilting lines on the bush and treetop, because they will be stuffed later.

6. To cut the batting and the backing, place the assembled house face down on each and trace around its outline. Make sure you add the required ¼-inch seam allowance. Cut out the backing and the batting.

7. Baste the top, batting and backing together.

8. Quilt on the marked lines until all lines have been completely stitched.

9. To finish the edges, trim away any excess

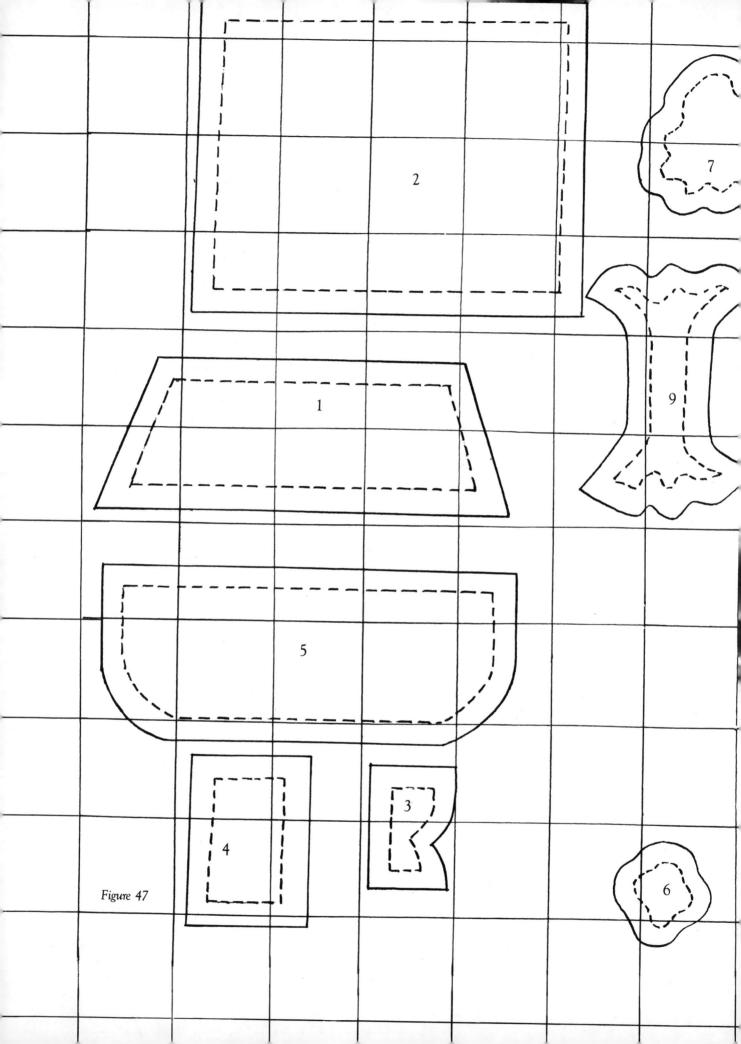

Figure 47

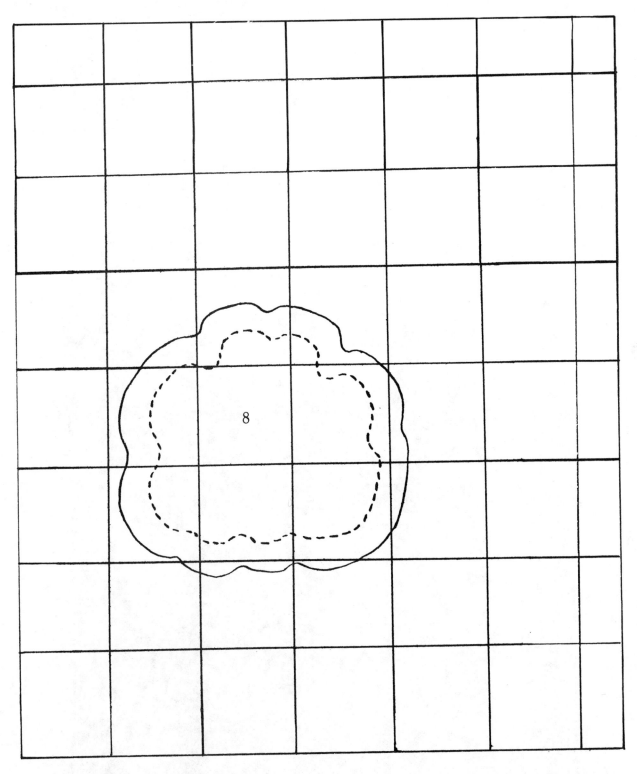

batting and whipstitch the folded edges of the top and the backing together neatly. Now stuff the treetop and the bush, both quite fully, and close up the openings.

10. To hang the house, either attach a dowel to the top and the bottom with fabric loops or sew a piece of ribbon across the middle of the back to form a hanger.

Pillows

All three of these designs for pillow covers are variations on old quilt patterns. The first—the bride's quilt design—is all appliquéd, while the other two—the pine tree and the bear's paw—are both pieced *and* appliquéd. After the pillow tops are completed, all the covers are made in exactly the same way; you add batting and lining material to the top, quilt it, and then attach it to the back of he cover on three sides. After you have slipped in the pillow form, whipstitch the opening closed or, if you prefer, put in a zipper.

Bear's Paw

Size:
15 x 15 inches

Materials:
½ yard of off-white material, 36 inches wide, for the top and back of the pillow cover
½ yard of lining material, 36 inches wide
¼ yard each of two different print materials, 36 inches wide
Small roll of batting
Knife-edge pillow, 15-inch form
Cording for edges (optional)
Zipper (optional), 14-inch length

Appears in color on page 38

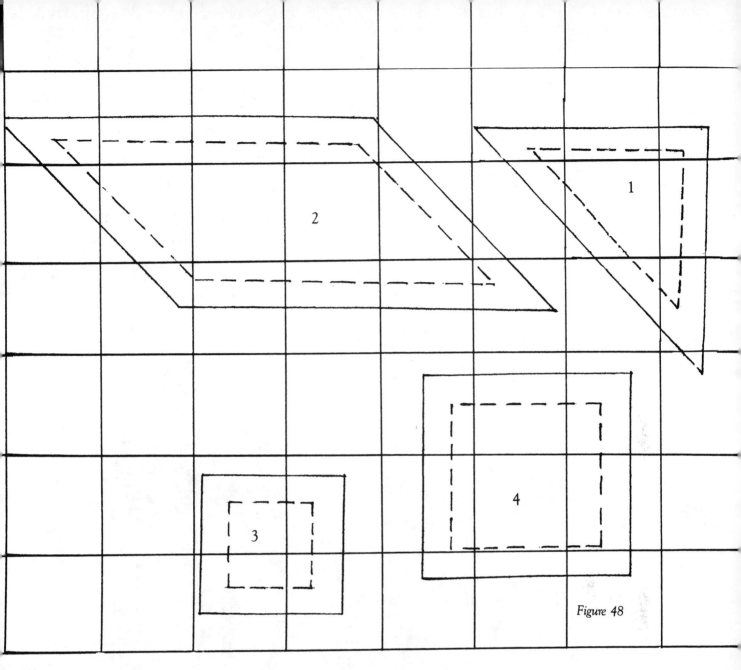

Figure 48

Directions:

1. Make a template for a 15½-inch square. Mark a ¼-inch seam allowance on it. Cut four squares—two from the off-white fabric for the front and the back, one from the batting and one from the lining material. Transfer seam lines to each piece.

2. Make templates for each of the four different parts of the design and mark on each how many to cut and from which fabric. You will need to cut eight of #1 and eight of #2 (both from the same print material), one of #3 and four of #4 (both from the other print material). Transfer all seam lines to each piece.

3. Study the illustration on page 124 carefully and note how the different pieces fit together. First join the slanted ends of #2 together to form the four L-shaped pieces of the design. Now piece #4 to the inside square corner of the L. Next, add #1 to the two other sides of #4.

4. In the exact center of the pillow-cover top, appliqué #3. Now appliqué the pieced paws at each corner of #3, making sure the paws are perpendicular to the center square. Check the illustration on page 124 again to be sure of the placement.

5. Mark quilting lines on the completed top. I

suggest marking them around all parts of the design, both inside and outside.

6. Baste the top, batting and lining together.

7. Begin quilting in the center of the top and continue until all quilting lines are completed.

8. If you are adding cording to the outside edges of the pillow cover, do it now, following the instructions given on page 26. With right sides facing, baste the top and the back of the pillow together along the seam lines on three sides. Sew and remove the bastings. Turn right side out.

9. Insert the pillow form and fold in the raw edges of the remaining sides on both the back and the front of the pillow cover. Whipstitch together. If you prefer, you can insert a zipper to join the two edges.

Bride's Quilt

Size:
15 x 15 inches

Materials:
½ yard of off-white material, 36 inches wide, for the top and back of the pillow cover
½ yard of lining material, 36 inches wide
¼ yard of light green material, 36 inches wide
¼ yard of dark green material, 36 inches wide
⅛ yard of red material, 36 inches wide
Embroidery floss
Small roll of batting
Small amount of loose polyester stuffing
Knife-edge pillow, 15-inch form
Cording for edges (optional)
Zipper (optional), 14-inch length

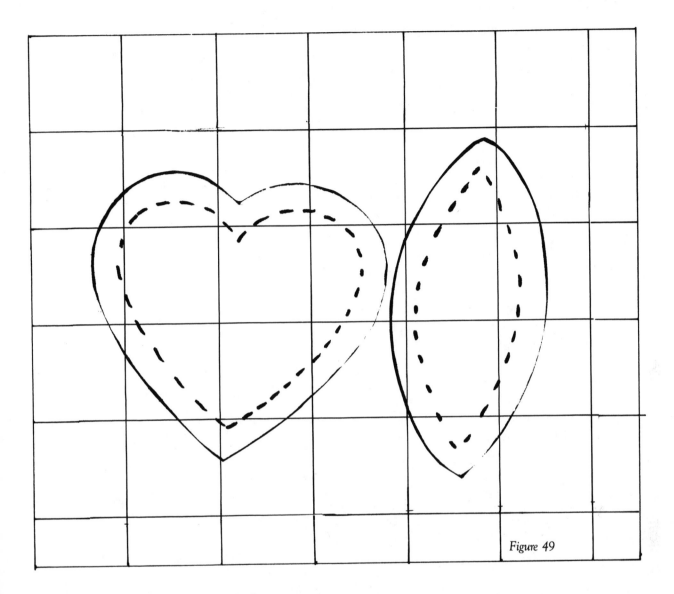

Figure 49

Directions:

1. Make a template for a 15½-inch square. Mark a ¼-inch seam allowance on it. Cut four squares—two from the off-white fabric for the front and the back, one from the batting, and one from the lining material. Transfer seam lines to each square.

2. Make templates for each of the two different parts of the design and mark on each how many to cut and from which fabric. You will need to cut eight hearts in all—six from the red fabric and two from the light green fabric—and twenty-seven leaves—thirteen from the light green fabric and fourteen from the dark green fabric. Transfer seam and accent lines to each piece.

3. Study the illustration on page 126 carefully and note where the hearts and leaves are placed. The circular stem which surrounds the center hearts will be embroidered after all the pieces are appliquéd. Begin appliquéing the four center hearts—two in red and two in light green. Leave a small opening on the side of each to stuff lightly. Close up the openings after stuffing. Next, appliqué the hearts in the corners. You may want to stuff these hearts. If you do, be sure to close up the openings after stuffing. Now appliqué the leaves in a circle

around the center hearts, alternating dark and light green leaves. You may also stuff some or all of these leaves if you like. Be sure to close up the openings after stuffing. Now embroider the stem that connects the leaves in the stem stitch.

4. Mark quilting lines on the completed pillow top. I suggest an outline pattern around all parts of the design.

5. Now baste the top, batting and lining material together.

6. Begin quilting in the center of the top and continue until all quilting lines are completed.

7. If you are adding cording to the outside edges of the pillow cover, do it now, following the instructions given on page 26. With right sides facing, baste the top and the back of the pillow cover together along the seam lines on three sides. Sew and remove the bastings. Turn the cover right side out.

8. Insert the pillow form, fold in the raw edges of the remaining sides of both the front and the back and whipstitch together. If you prefer, you can insert a zipper to join the two edges.

Pine Tree

Size:
15 x 15 inches

Materials:
½ yard of plain-colored material, 36 inches wide, for the top and back of the pillow cover
½ yard of lining material, 36 inches wide
Large scraps of plain-colored and print materials
Small roll of batting
Knife-edge pillow, 15-inch form
Cording for edges (optional)
Zipper (optional), 14-inch length

Directions:

1. Make a template for a 15½-inch square. Mark a ¼-inch seam allowance on it. Cut four squares—two from the plain-colored fabric for the front and the back, one from the batting and one from the lining material. Transfer seam lines to each square.

2. Make templates for each of the four different parts of the design and mark on each how many to cut and from which fabric. You will need to cut one tree trunk (#1), one treetop (#2), ten leaves (#3) and two of the base of the tree (#4)—one from print fabric and one from plain-colored fabric. Transfer seam lines to each piece.

3. Study the illustration on page 129 carefully to see how the design pieces fit together. Appliqué the tree trunk (#1) first. Next, appliqué the treetop (#2), making sure it is centered at the top of the tree trunk. Now appliqué the bases (#4) on either side of the trunk. Finally, appliqué the leaves (#3) in position at the points of the treetop.

4. Mark the quilting lines. I suggest using an outline pattern around all parts of the design. Repeat the outline pattern for the inside of the treetop and, if you like, on the open spaces outside of the design.

5. Now baste the top, batting and lining material together.

6. Begin quilting in the center of the top and continue until all quilting lines are completely stitched.

7. If you are adding cording to the outside edges of the pillow cover, do it now, following the instructions given on page 26. With right sides facing, baste the quilted top and the back of the pillow cover along the seam lines on three sides. Sew and remove the bastings. Turn the cover right side out.

8. Insert the pillow form, fold in the raw edges of the remaining sides of both the front and the back and whipstitch together. If you prefer, you can insert a zipper to join the two edges.

Appears in color on page 38

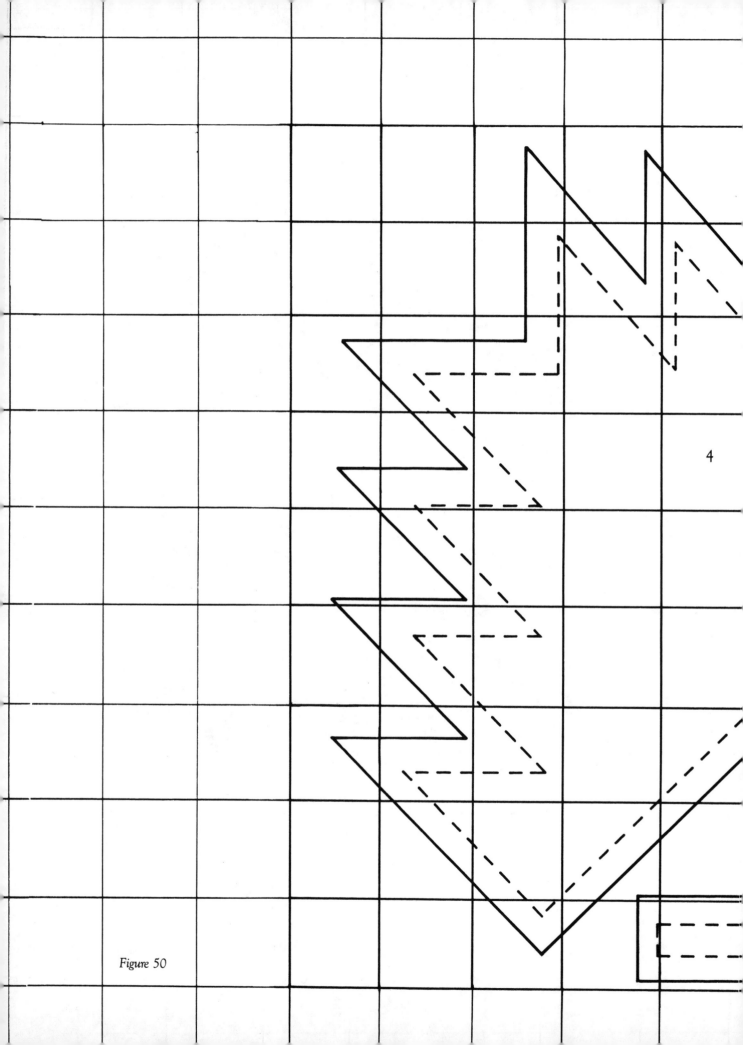

Figure 50

4

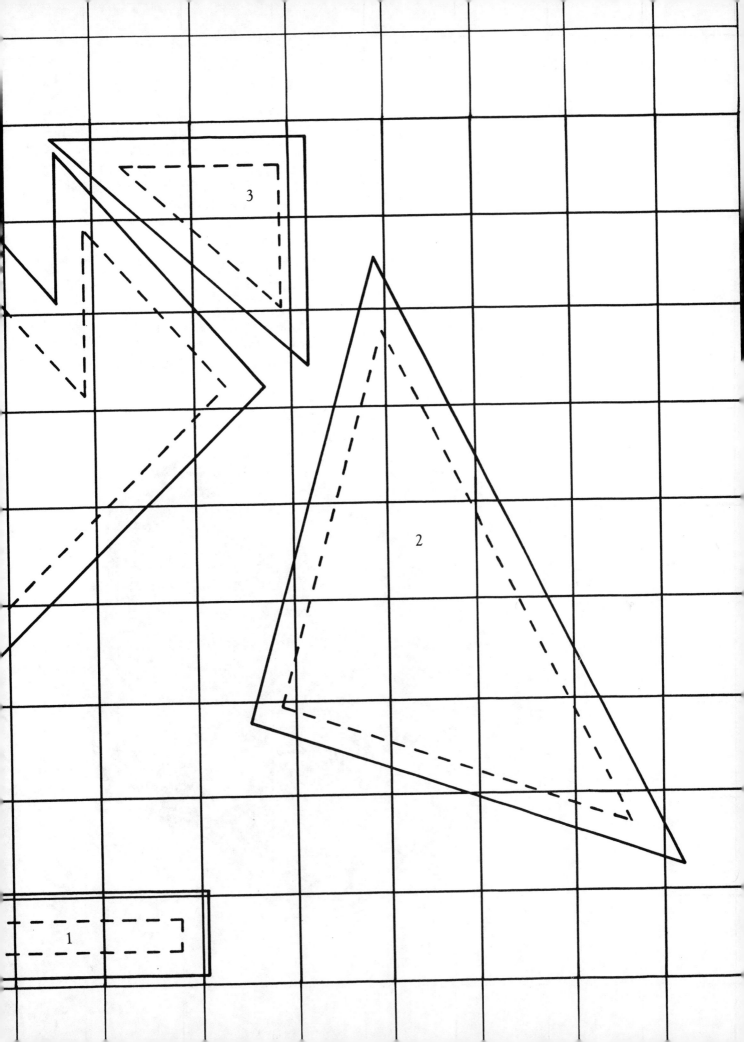

1

2

3

Pincushions

Sewing accessories like these two pincushions and needle-book are fun and easy to make. I not only stuff my pincushions, but fill the bottoms with sand; this way they sit well on a flat surface, and the sand keeps my needles and pins sharp.

Scallop

Size:
5 inches in diameter

Materials:
¼ yard of plain-colored material, 36 inches wide, for the top and the back of the pincushion
Scraps of material for the flower design
Small amount of batting
Small amount of loose polyester stuffing
Embroidery floss
A cup of white sand (available at garden or hardware stores)

Directions:
1. Make templates for the two parts of the design. Mark on each how many to cut and from which material. You will need to cut four

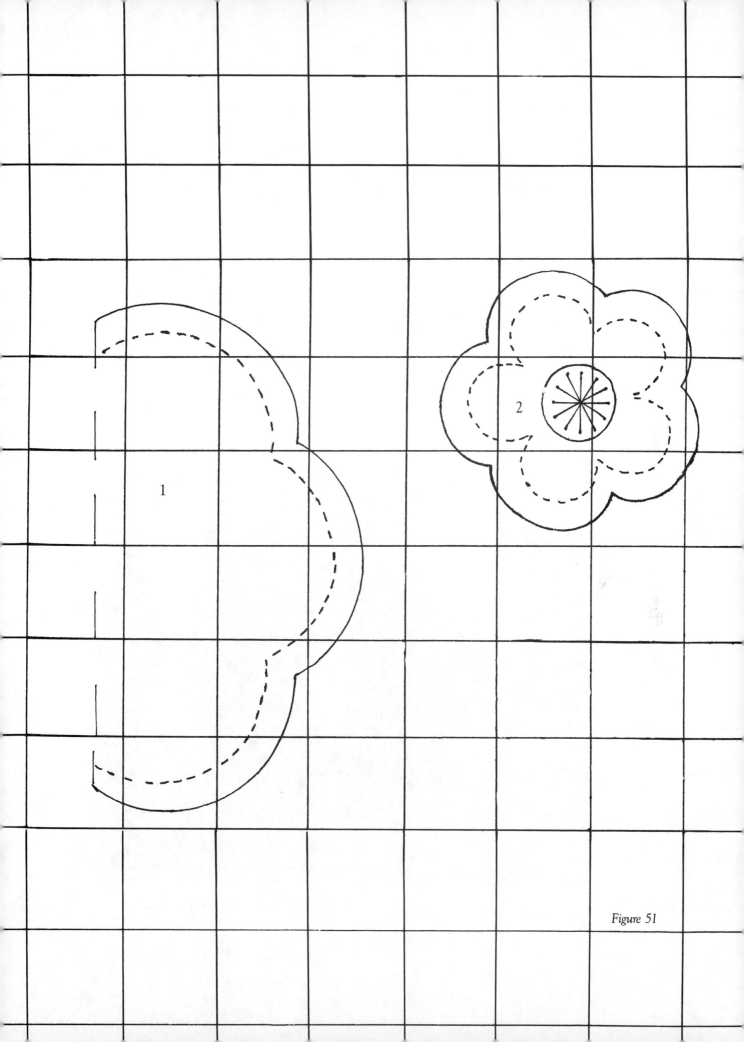

Figure 51

of the pincushion (#1)—three from the plain-colored fabric and one from the batting. (Note that all of these must be cut on the fold of the material.) You will also need to cut one of the flower (#2). Transfer seam and accent lines to each piece.

2. Embroider the center of the flower (#2) with the chain stitch, following the accent lines, or fill it in with the satin stitch.

3. Appliqué the flower (#2) onto the center of the top of the pincushion (#1), and leave an opening. Stuff the flower quite fully and close up the opening.

4. Mark quilting lines on the top, outlining the flower design.

5. Assemble the top of the pincushion by basting the top, batting and backing together. Quilt the marked quilting lines.

6. If you wish to trim the edges with cording, as shown in the illustration, attach the cording before joining the front and back. See instructions on page 26. Fold under the outside seam allowances on both the front and the back of the pincushion, and baste together, wrong sides facing. Sew, either by hand or machine, leaving a small opening on one side to stuff. Remove bastings.

7. Stuff the pincushion very fully and firmly. Pour in the cup of sand so that it will fall to the bottom of the pincushion. Whipstitch the opening tightly closed so the grains of sand will not escape.

Needle-Book

Size:
3½ x 6½ inches

Materials:
⅛ yard of plain-colored material, 36 inches wide
Scraps of material for the design

Small piece of batting
Small amount of loose polyester stuffing
Embroidery floss

Directions:

1. Make a template for each of the two parts of the design. Cut three of the needle-book (#4)—two from the plain-colored fabric for the top and the lining, and one from the batting. (Note that these will all be cut on the fold of the material.) You will also need to cut one of the flower (#2) from page 133. Transfer seam and accent lines to each piece.
2. Embroider the center of the flower (#2) with the chain stitch, following the accent lines, or fill in the center with the satin stitch.
3. Appliqué the flower (#2) to the center of the top of the needle-book (#4). (Since this needle-book is folded, only one half is the top.) Leave an opening on its side for stuffing. Stuff the flower very fully and close up the opening.
4. Mark quilting lines only on the top of the needle-book. Use an outline pattern around the flower.
5. Baste the three layers of the needle-book together—the top and back, the batting and the lining—but quilt only on the marked lines around the flower on the top.
6. Fold under the outside seam allowance on both the top and the lining, and whipstitch the edges together, wrong sides facing.
7. Now fold it in half to form the completed needle-book.

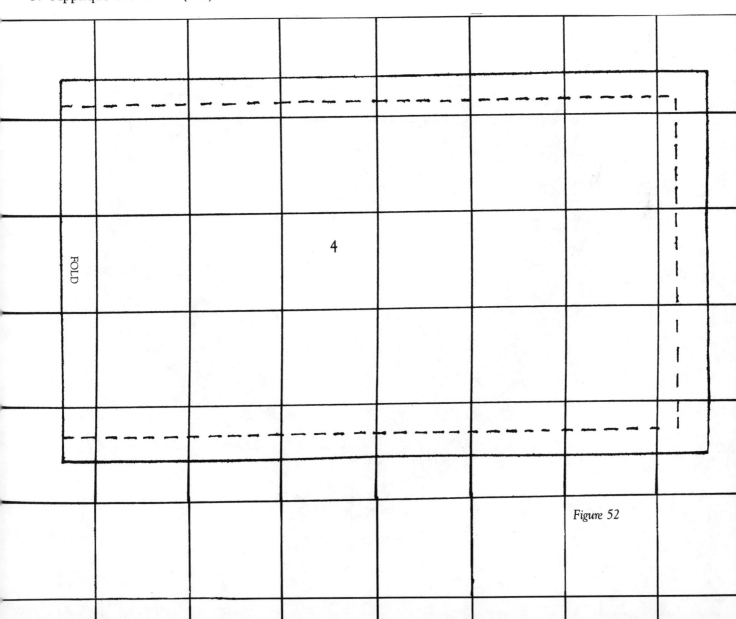

FOLD

4

Figure 52

Heart

Size:
5½ x 6½ inches

Materials:
¼ yard of plain red material, 36 inches wide, for the top and back of the pincushion
Scraps of plain rose and pale pink material
Small amount of loose polyester stuffing
A cup of white sand (available at garden or hardware stores)

Directions:
1. Make templates for each of the three different parts of the design and mark on each how many to cut and from what fabric. You will need to cut two of the largest heart (#1) from the plain red fabric, one of the middle-sized heart (#2) from the rose fabric and one of the smallest heart (#3) from the pale pink fabric. Transfer all seam lines to each piece.
2. Appliqué heart #2 to the largest heart (#1), making sure to center it exactly. Now appliqué the smallest heart (#3) to the center of heart #2, again making sure to center it exactly.
3. Fold under the outside seam allowances on both of the large red hearts (#1) and baste together along the seam lines, wrong sides facing. Whipstitch the two edges together, leaving an opening on the side of the heart to stuff. Stuff the pincushion very fully and firmly.
4. Now pour in the sand so it will fall on the bottom of the pincushion. Whipstitch the opening securely closed so the grains of sand will not escape.

Appears in color on page 33

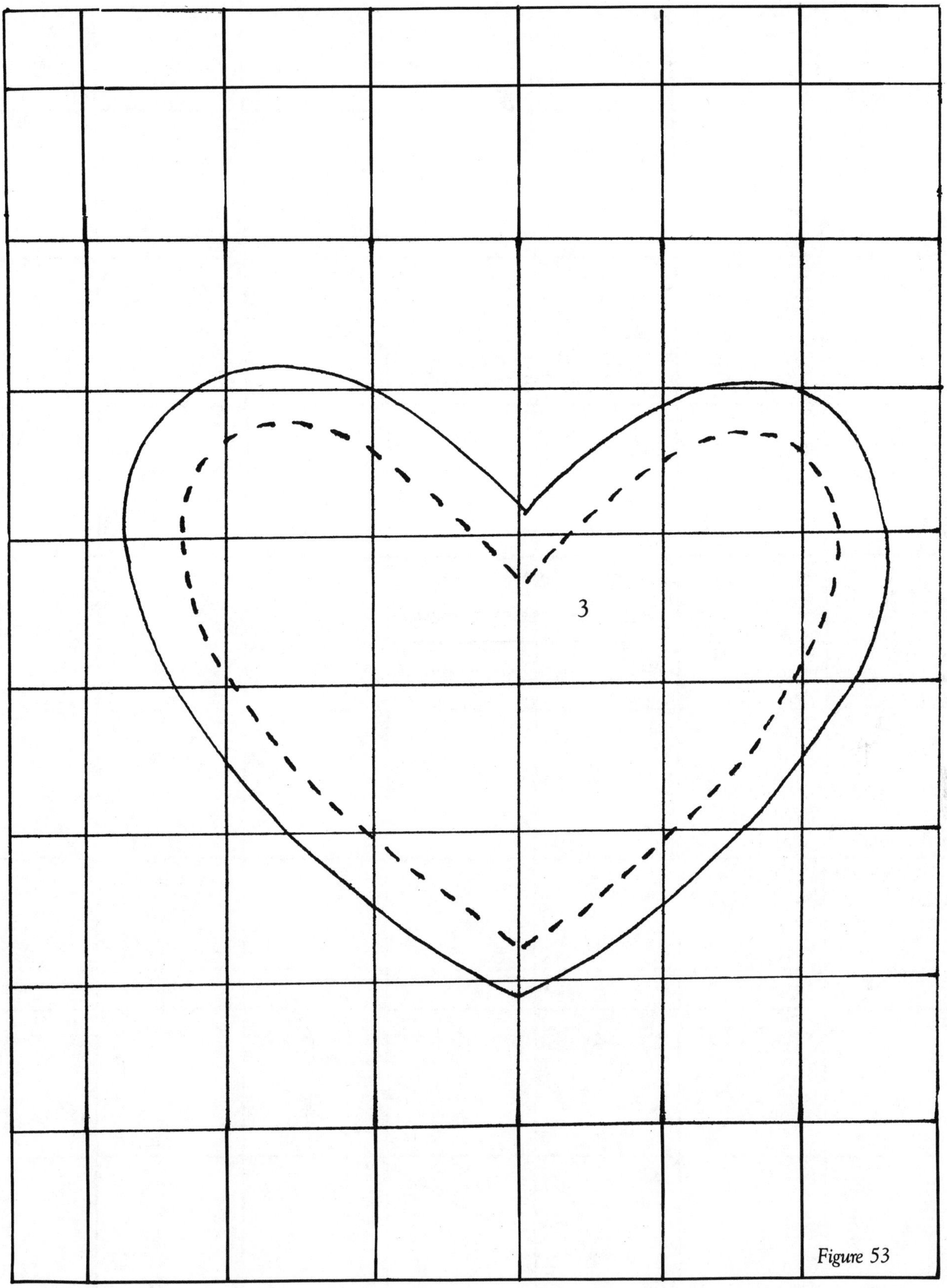

3

Figure 53

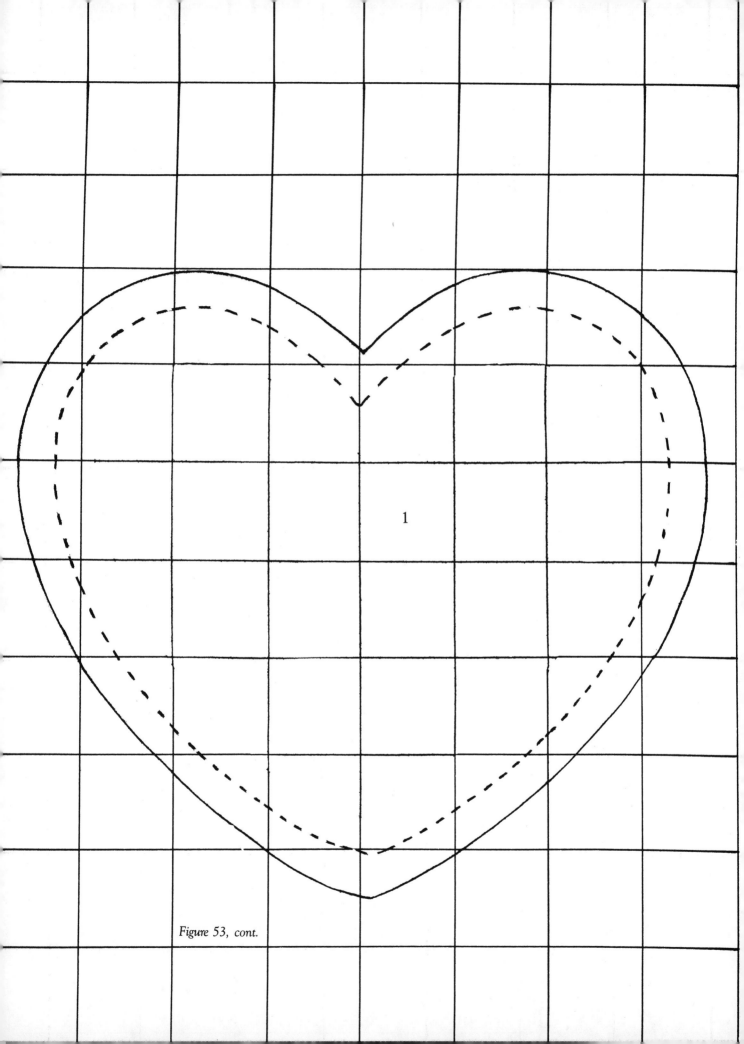

Figure 53, cont.

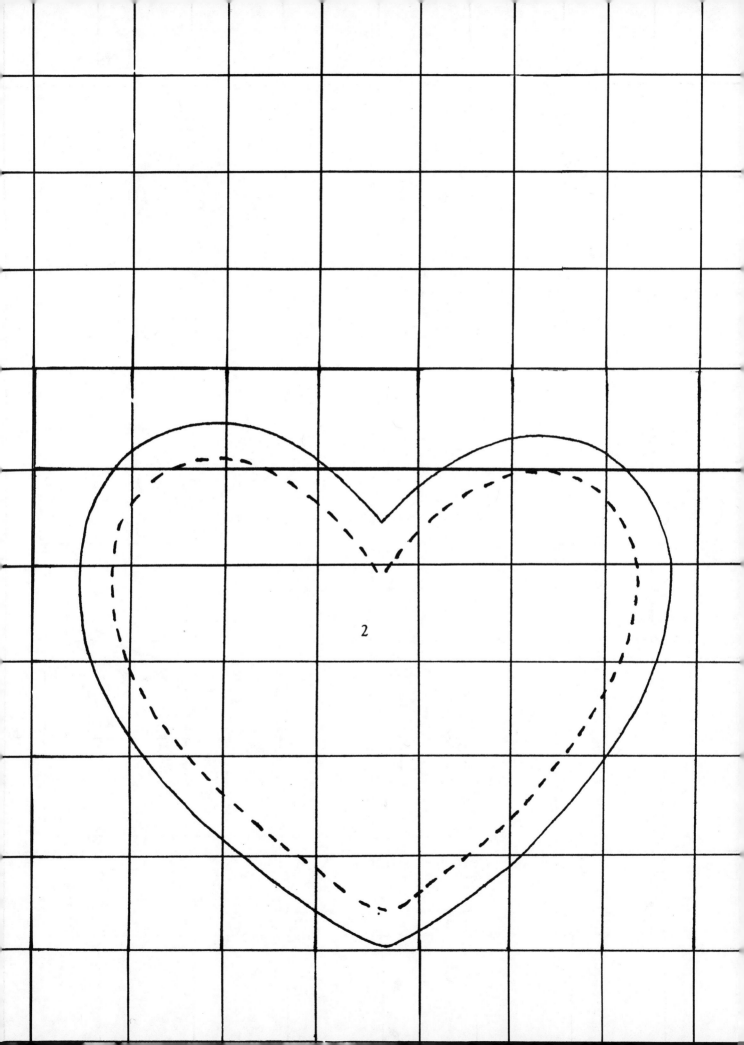

2

Christmas Decorations

Here are eight different designs for hanging Christmas decorations. All have been taken from traditional quilt designs and adapted for stuffing and hanging, so there is no reason to save them just for the Christmas tree. I think they make marvelous toys to hang over a crib or on the side of a playpen. They are all very simple to make and give you a chance to use up some of those scraps of fabric that are too big to throw away but too small for anything else.

Pine Tree

Materials:
Scraps of plain-colored and print material
Small amount of loose polyester stuffing

Directions:
1. Make templates for both parts of the design and mark on each how many to cut and from which fabric. You will need two of #1 and two of #2.
2. Cut out the pieces and transfer the seam lines to each piece.
3. Turn under the seam allowances of all parts, and then baste the trunk (#2) to the base of #1, as shown in the illustration above. Do the same for the back.

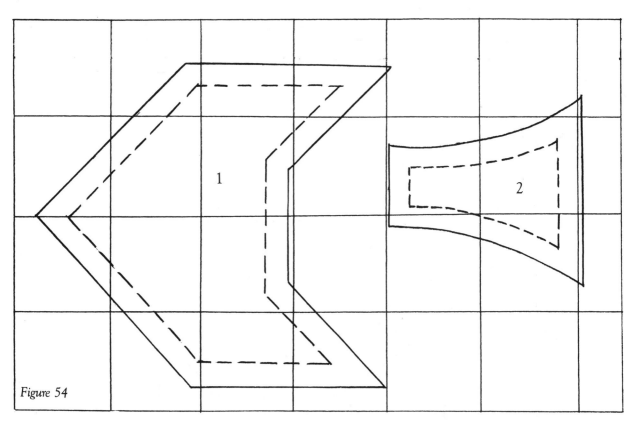

Figure 54

4. Place the back and the front together, wrong sides facing, and whipstitch the folded edges. Leave an opening for stuffing.

5. Stuff the decoration very firmly and fully. Before closing up the opening, attach a string with a loop at the end for hanging. Whipstitch the opening closed.

Prairie Flower

Materials:
Scraps of plain-colored and print material
Embroidery floss
Small amount of loose polyester stuffing

Directions:
1. Make templates for both parts of the design. Cut two of each.
2. Cut out the pieces and transfer seam and accent lines to each piece.
3. In the center of the flower (#2), embroider five French knots very close together to form a center.

4. Turn under the seam allowance on all pieces. Appliqué #2 on the center of #1.
5. Place the front and the back of the decoration together, wrong sides facing, and whipstitch the folded edges. Leave an opening at the top for stuffing.
6. Stuff the decoration very fully and firmly. Before closing up the opening, attach a string with a loop at the end for hanging. Close up the opening by whipstitching.

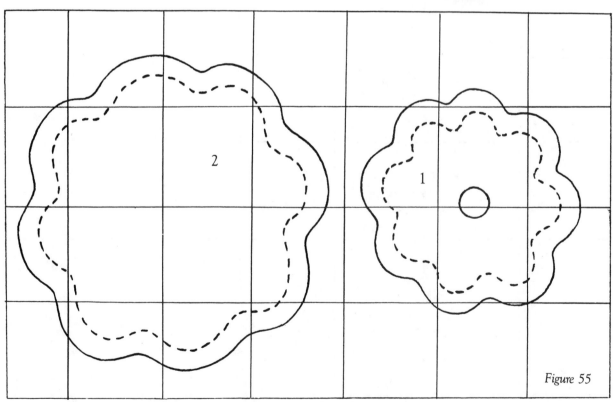

Figure 55

Grandmother's Flower Garden

Materials:
Scraps of plain-colored and print material
Small amount of loose polyester stuffing

Directions:
1. Make templates for both parts of the design and mark on each how many to cut and from which fabric. You will need twelve of #1, six of the print material and six of the plain.
2. Cut out all pieces of the design, and transfer seam lines to each piece.
3. Study the illustration at right to see how the design is assembled. This picture shows the front of the decoration. Beginning at the point in the center and working toward the outside, join a print diamond to a plain-colored diamond. Repeat this procedure, alternating

print and plain, until all six parts of the front have been joined. Do the same for the back. Press the seams to one side.
4. Turn under the outside seam allowances of both the front and the back, and, with wrong sides together, whipstitch the folded edges of

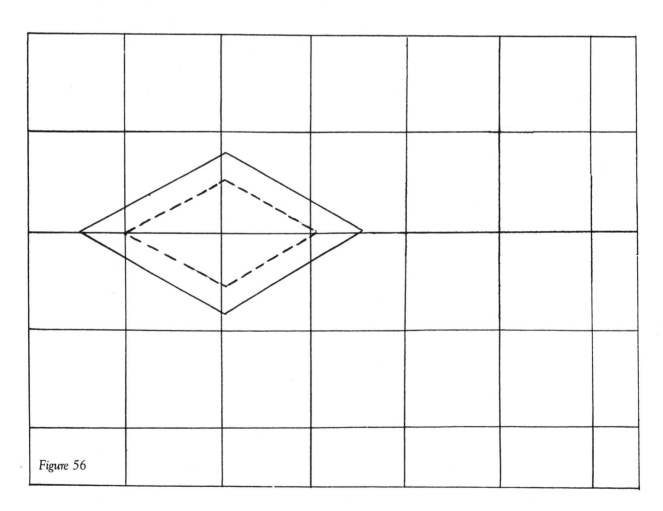

Figure 56

both sides together. Be sure to leave an opening for stuffing.

5. Now stuff the decoration very firmly and fully. Before closing the opening, attach a string with a loop at the end for hanging. Close the opening by whipstitching.

Bird of Paradise

Materials:
Scraps of plain-colored or print material
Small amount of loose polyester stuffing

Directions:
1. Make a template for the one piece in this design, and cut two from your fabric. Transfer the seam lines.
2. Turn under the seam allowance on both

pieces and place them together, wrong sides facing. Whipstitch the folded edges, leaving an opening at the beak for stuffing.

3. Stuff the decoration very firmly and fully. Before closing up the opening, attach a string with a loop at the end for hanging. Close up the opening by whipstitching.

Appears in color on page 37

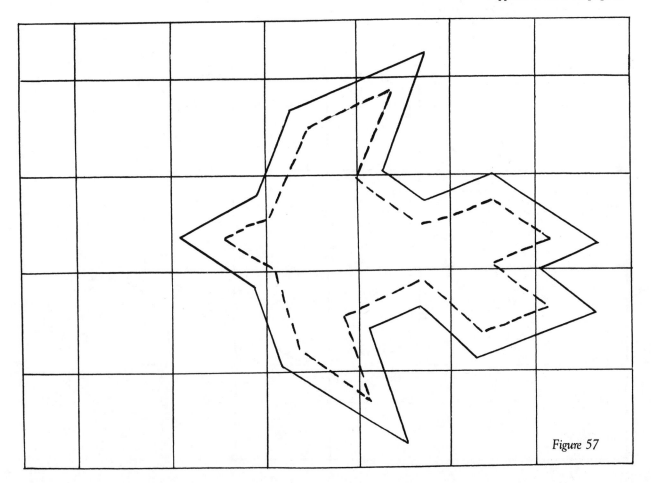

Figure 57

Prairie Rose

Materials:
Scraps of green, red and print material
Small amount of loose polyester stuffing

Directions:
1. Make templates for each of the three different parts of the design. Mark on each how many to cut and from which fabric. You will need two of #1, six of #2 and two of #3.
2. Cut out all the pieces of the design and transfer seam lines to each piece.
3. Appliqué the center circle (#3) to #1. Do this for both the front and the back of the decoration. Now appliqué the leaves (#2) in the proper position on both the front and the back.
4. Place the front and the back together, wrong sides facing, and whipstitch the folded edges. Be sure to leave an opening at the top.
5. Now stuff the decoration very fully and firmly. Before closing up the opening, attach a string with a loop at the top for hanging. Whipstitch the opening closed.

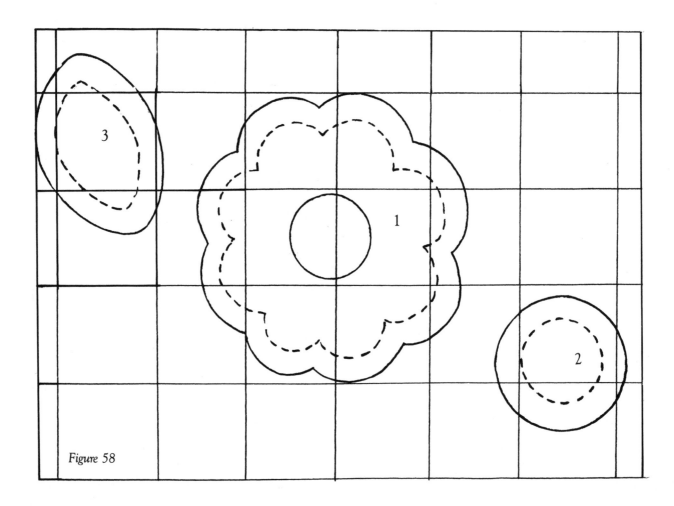

Figure 58

Butterfly

Materials:
Scraps of plain-colored and print material
Small amount of loose polyester stuffing

Directions:
1. Make templates for both parts of the design. Cut two of each.
2. Cut out the pieces and transfer seam and accent lines to both.
3. Turn under the seam allowance on all pieces. Baste #2 to the base of #1, as shown in the illustration. Whipstitch the two pieces together. Do the same for the back.
4. Place the front and back together, wrong sides facing, and whipstitch the folded outer edges. Leave an opening at the top for stuffing.
5. Stuff the decoration very fully and firmly, and close up the opening securely.
6. Attach a string to the decoration, as shown in the illustration, to form a hanging loop at the end of the string.

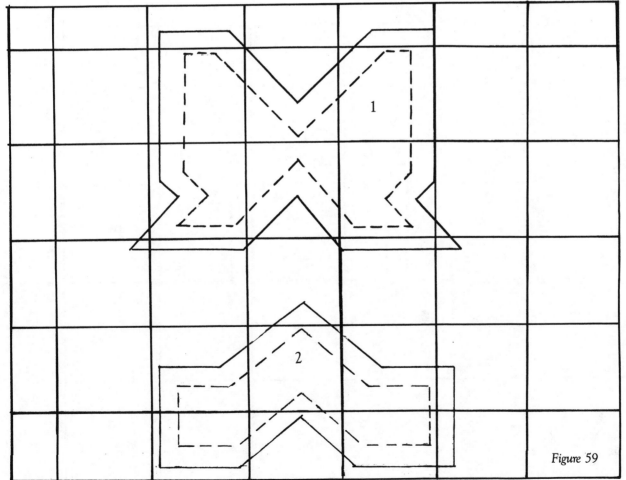

Figure 59

Snowflake

Materials:
Scraps of two different plain colors and either white or print for the center
Small amount of loose polyester stuffing

Directions:
1. Make a template for the two different parts of the design and mark on it how many to cut from each fabric. You will need two for the center from the white or print fabric, six cut from one of the plain colors, and six cut from the other plain color.
2. Cut out all the pieces, and transfer seam lines to each piece.
3. Study the illustration to see how to alternate the two plain-colored pieces. Begin joining first one color and then the other to the

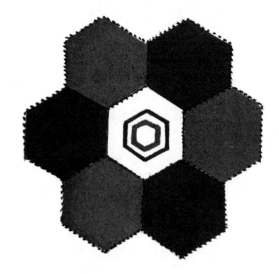

center piece. When all have been attached, join the sides together. Do this in exactly the same way for the back. Press all seams open to make a smooth design.
4. Turn under the outside edges of both the

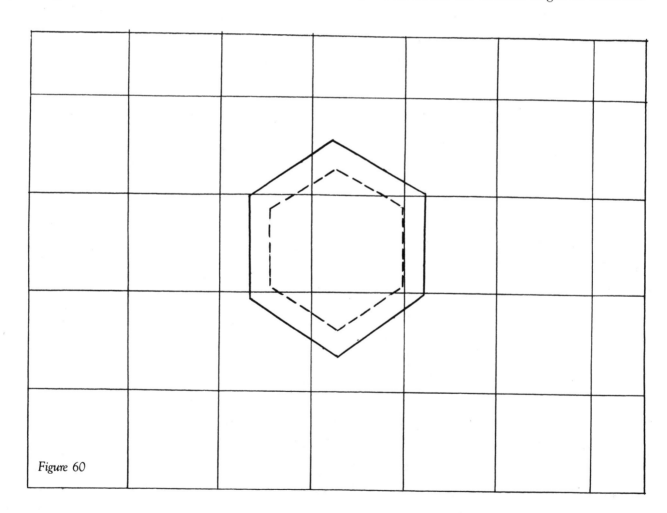

Figure 60

front and the back. Place the front and back together, wrong sides facing, and whipstitch the folded edges. Leave an opening at the top for stuffing.

5. Stuff the decoration very firmly and fully. Before closing up the opening attach a string with a hanging loop at the end.

pieces, and place them together, wrong sides facing. Whipstitch the folded edges, leaving an opening at the bottom for stuffing.

3. Stuff the decoration fully and firmly. Before closing up the opening, attach a string with a loop for hanging at the end.

Indian Arrow

Materials:
Scraps of print material
Small amount of loose polyester stuffing

Directions:
1. Make a template for the one part of this design. Cut out two pieces from your fabric and transfer the seam lines.
2. Turn under the seam allowance on both

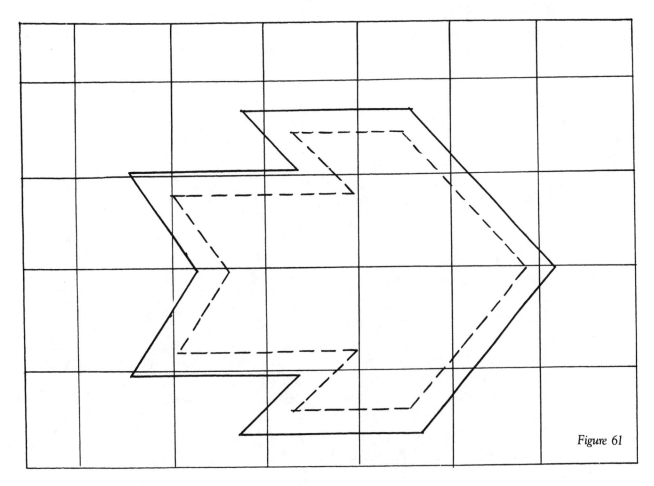

Figure 61

6. Designs for the Kitchen

Tea Cozies

I like tea, and I like tea cozies, because they keep my tea hot and look so cheerful in the kitchen even when I'm not using my teapot. Here are two designs—an elflike tiger and a three-dimensional cottage—that I am particularly fond of.

Tiger

Size:
7 x 9½ inches

Materials:
½ yard of orange, rust or tan material, 36 inches wide, for the outside of the tea cozy
½ yard of lining material, 36 inches wide
Embroidery floss
Small roll of batting
Small amount of loose polyester stuffing
Bias tape

Directions:
1. Make templates for each of the three parts of the tiger. Cut two of each part—one each for the front and the back. Reverse each of the templates when you are marking the second outline. Transfer seam and accent lines to each piece.
2. Embroider the accent lines on the tiger's head (#2); use the satin stitch for the eyes, nose, ears and mouth, and the chain or stem stitch for the whiskers and other lines. Do this for both the front and the back. Also using the satin stitch, embroider the accent lines on the tail (#3) and the body (#1); do this for both the front and the back.
3. Appliqué the head (#2) in place on the body (#1), making sure it extends somewhat beyond the edge of the body. Check the illustration opposite for its position. Next, appliqué the tail (#3) on the body. Leave an opening at the upper side of the tail and stuff it lightly. Close up the opening.
4. Mark quilting lines on both the front and the back. I suggest outlining the parts of the face—eyes, nose, ears, mouth and whiskers—and then marking wavy lines about ¼ inch apart on the rest of the face. This gives the tiger a nice weather-beaten look. For the rest of the body, mark curved or wavy lines.
5. Now cut out the batting and lining pieces for both the front and the back. To do this, place the finished tiger face down on the batting, and trace around its outline twice. Do the same on the lining material. Cut out the pieces of batting and lining, and mark the ¼-inch seam allowance.
6. Baste together the three parts for one side of the tea cozy—the appliquéd front, the batting and the lining. Do the same for the back.

7. Quilt both the front and the back.

8. Now join the front and the back of the tea cozy by basting the two together, right sides facing, along the outside seam lines. Do not baste the bottom edges. Sew along the basted lines, being careful to reinforce your stitching at the bottom edges. Remove bastings.

9. Cut a length of bias tape that will fit exactly the distance from the bottom of the front paws, up over the back and down to the other bottom edge. Sew the tape over the raw edges. Turn the tea cozy right side out.

10. Finish the tea cozy by covering the bottom edges with bias tape.

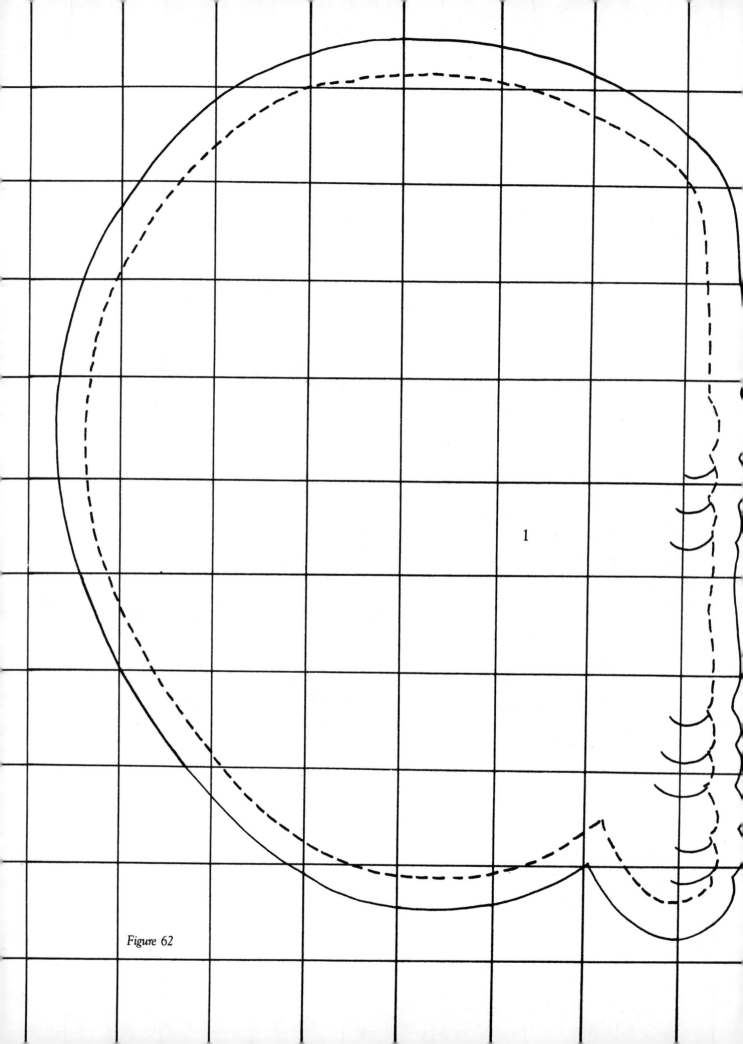

1

Figure 62

Canary Cottage

Size:
11 x 9 x 5 inches

Materials:
½ yard of yellow material, 36 inches wide
⅛ yard of red material, 36 inches wide
Scraps of material, including a plain green color and a green-and-white print
½ yard of lining material, 36 inches wide
Embroidery floss
Small roll of batting
Bias binding

Directions:
1. Make templates for each of the nine different parts of the design. Enlarge them, using 2-inch squares rather than the 1-inch squares as given. Mark on each how many to cut and from which fabric. Cut six of the roof (#1)—two from the red material, two from the batting and two from the lining fabric. Cut six of the house (#2)—two from the yellow material, two from the batting and two from the lining fabric. Cut six of the chimney (#6)—two from scraps of fabric, two from the batting and two from the lining fabric. Cut six of the side (#8)—two from the yellow material, two from the batting and two from the lining fabric. Cut six of the peak (#9)—two from the yellow material, two from the batting and two from the lining fabric. Cut two of the door (#4) and twelve of the curtain (#5) from scraps of material, remembering to reverse the template when marking the last six. Cut twelve of the shutters (#3) from scraps of green fabric and four of the bush (#7) from the green-and-white print material. Transfer seam and accent lines to all pieces.
2. Appliqué the door (#4) to both the front and the back of the house (#2), making sure to center it. Next, appliqué the curtains (#5) on the front, back and sides of the house, touching the points together at the top and bottom to form the window. Now appliqué the shutters (#3) to the sides of the windows on the front, back and sides of the house. Finally, appliqué the bushes (#7) to the front and back of the house.
3. Now do the embroidery work. Use a French knot for the doorknob on the door (#4) and a chain stitch for the inside parts of the door. Use the outline stitch for the slat lines on the shutters (#3) and for the lines to form the window panes between the curtains (#5).
4. Mark the quilting lines on the various parts of the house. Use a brick design for the chimney, use shingle lines for the roof, and use clapboard lines for the house and sides. You might also like to outline the bushes, doors and windows.
5. Now assemble the various layers for each part of the house. Place the roof (#1) face down, place its batting on top of it, and, finally, place the roof lining on top of that, right side up. Baste the three layers together on the outside seam lines. Do the same for the house (#2), the chimney (#6), the sides (#8) and the peak (#9).
6. Quilt all quilting lines on all parts of the house.
7. Now join the various parts to form the house, first basting and then sewing them together. Follow this sequence: With right sides together, join one side of the house (#8) to a side (#2). Join the other side of #8 to the other house (#2). Now join the back of the house to the other two sides, again with right sides together. Now join the two roofs (#1) at the top. Next, join the peaks (#9) to the sides of the roof (#1). Finally, join the roof and peaks to the house and sides, again making sure all raw edges are turned to the inside.
8. On the inside of the house, bind all the raw edges with bias tape.
9. Turn the house to the right side and finish the raw bottom edges with bias tape.

Appears in color on page 33

10. Now join the two parts of the chimney by turning under all seam allowances and whipstitching the two parts together. Whipstitch the chimney in position on the roof of the house.

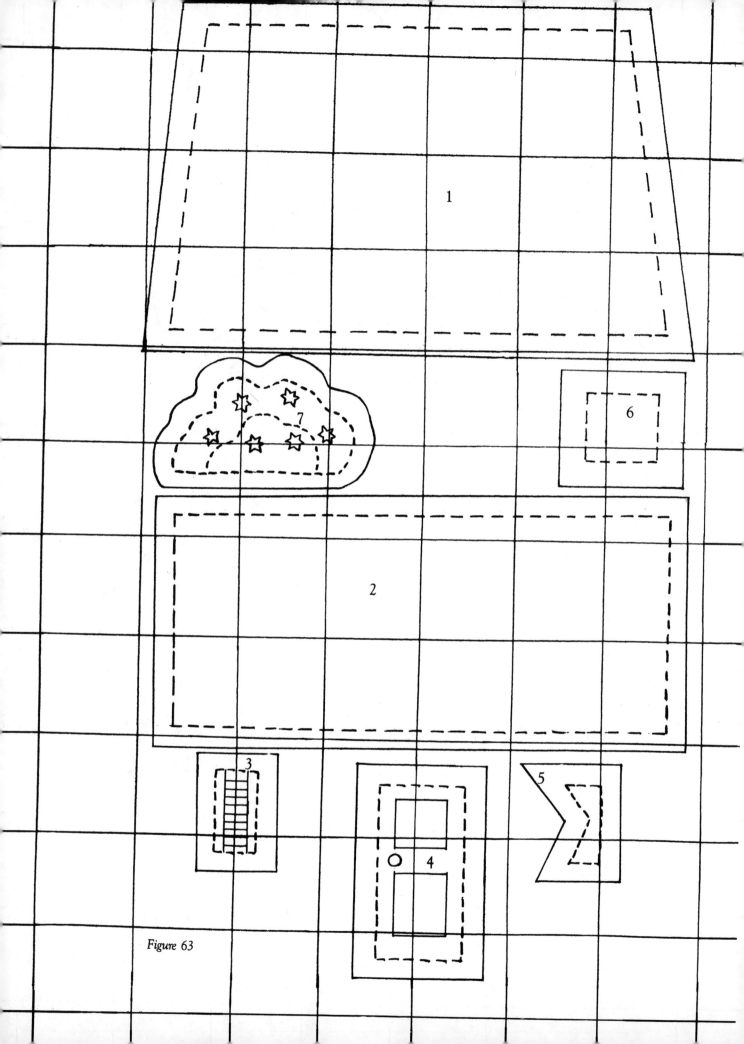

Figure 63

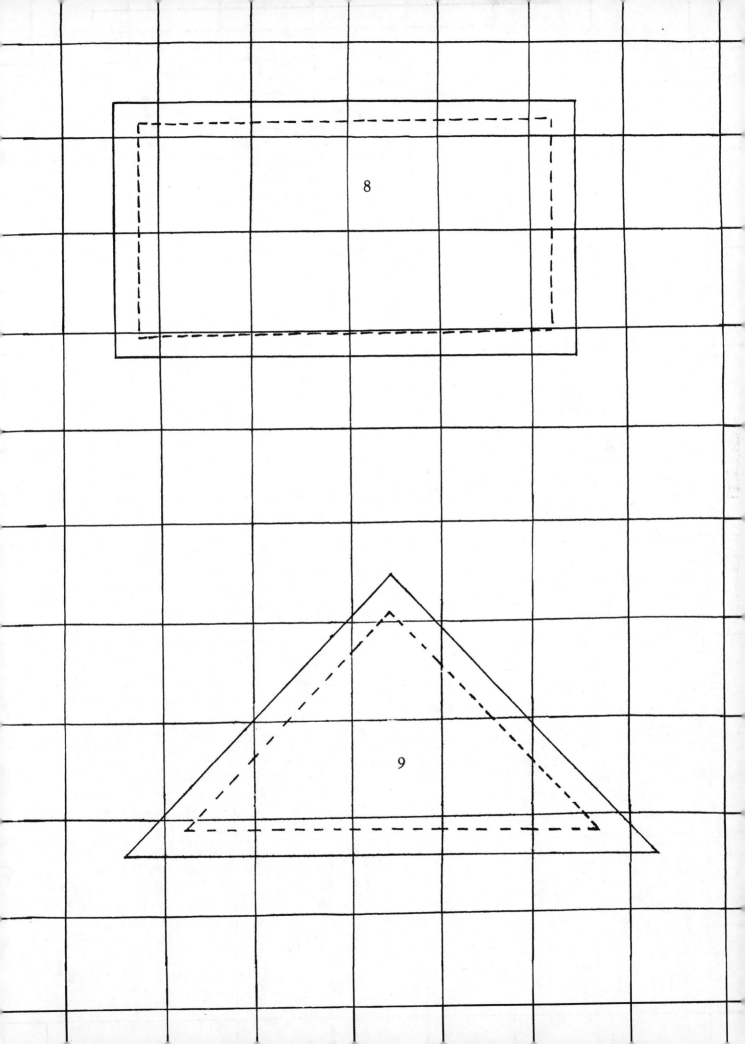

8

9

Appears in color on page 37

Toaster Covers

A quilted toaster cover with an attractive design appliquéd on its side makes good sense either for your own kitchen or for a new bride's. Here are two simple-to-make designs, as well as instructions for constructing the cover itself. The template pattern for the cover will easily fit over most ordinary toasters, but if yours is much larger or much smaller, measure it and make your own pattern.

Carrots

Size:
14 x 9 x 8 inches

Materials:
½ yard of plain-colored material, 36 inches wide, for front, back and center panel of the cover
½ yard of lining material, 36 inches wide
Scraps of orange and green material for the carrots
Small roll of batting
Small amount of loose polyester stuffing
Bias tape

Directions:
1. Make templates for the toaster cover. Enlarge the template in Figure 64 by using 2-inch squares, rather than the 1-inch squares as given. Cut two of the side of the cover (#1) and a long strip for the center panel from the plain material, the batting and the lining fabric. Transfer seam lines to each piece.
2. Make templates for the carrot design. You will need to cut three of the carrot (#2) from the orange scraps and three of the stalks from the green scraps—one of the short stalk (#3) and two of the longer stalks (#4). Transfer seam lines to each piece.
3. Appliqué the carrots on one side of the cover. Check the illustration above to see how they overlap. Leave a small opening on the side of the top carrot and stuff it lightly. Close up the opening. Now appliqué the short stalk (#3) in place, leaving an opening to stuff it lightly. Close up the opening. Finally, appliqué the longer stalks (#4) and stuff them slightly more. Close up the opening.
4. Now mark quilting lines on the front. Use an outline pattern around all parts of the carrot design and either diagonal or perpendicular lines for the rest of the front. Also, mark quilting lines—either diagonal or perpendicular lines—on the back and the center panel.
5. Now assemble the three layers for the front of the cover—the top, the batting and the lining—and baste them together. Do the same for the back and the center panel.
6. Quilt each of the three parts, always beginning in the center and continuing until all quilting lines are completely stitched.

7. Now baste the center panel to the front and back of the cover along the outside seam lines, making sure the raw edges are on the outside. Sew securely and remove the bastings.

8. Cover all raw edges of the toaster cover, including the bottom edge, by sewing bias tape along them.

Eggplant

Size:
14 x 9 x 8 inches

Materials:
½ yard of plain-colored material, 36 inches wide, for front, back and center panel of the cover
½ yard of lining material, 36 inches wide
Scraps of material for the eggplant
Embroidery floss
Small roll of batting
Small amount of loose polyester stuffing
Bias tape

Directions:
1. Make templates for the toaster cover. Enlarge the template in Figure 64 by using 2-inch squares, rather than 1-inch squares as given. Cut two of the side of the cover (#1) and a long strip for the center panel from the plain material, the batting and the lining fabric. Transfer seam lines to each piece.

2. Make templates for the two different parts of the eggplant design. Cut one of each. Transfer seam and accent lines to each piece.

3. Embroider the accent on the eggplant (#5) in the satin stitch.

4. Appliqué the eggplant (#5) in place first, leaving an opening on one side to stuff it later. Now appliqué the stem (#6) at the top of the eggplant. Stuff the eggplant quite fully and firmly and close up the opening.

5. Mark quilting lines on the front. Use an outline pattern around the eggplant and either diagonal or perpendicular lines for the rest of the front. Also, mark quilting lines—either diagonal or perpendicular lines—on the back and the center panel.

6. Now assemble the three layers for the front of the cover—the top, the batting and the lining—and baste them together. Do the same for the back and the center panel.

7. Quilt each of the three parts, always beginning in the center and continuing until all quilting lines are completely stitched.

8. Now baste the center panel to the front and back of the cover along the outside seam lines, making sure the raw edges are on the outside. Sew securely and remove the bastings.

9. Cover all raw edges of the toaster cover, including the bottom edge, by sewing bias tape along them.

Figure 64

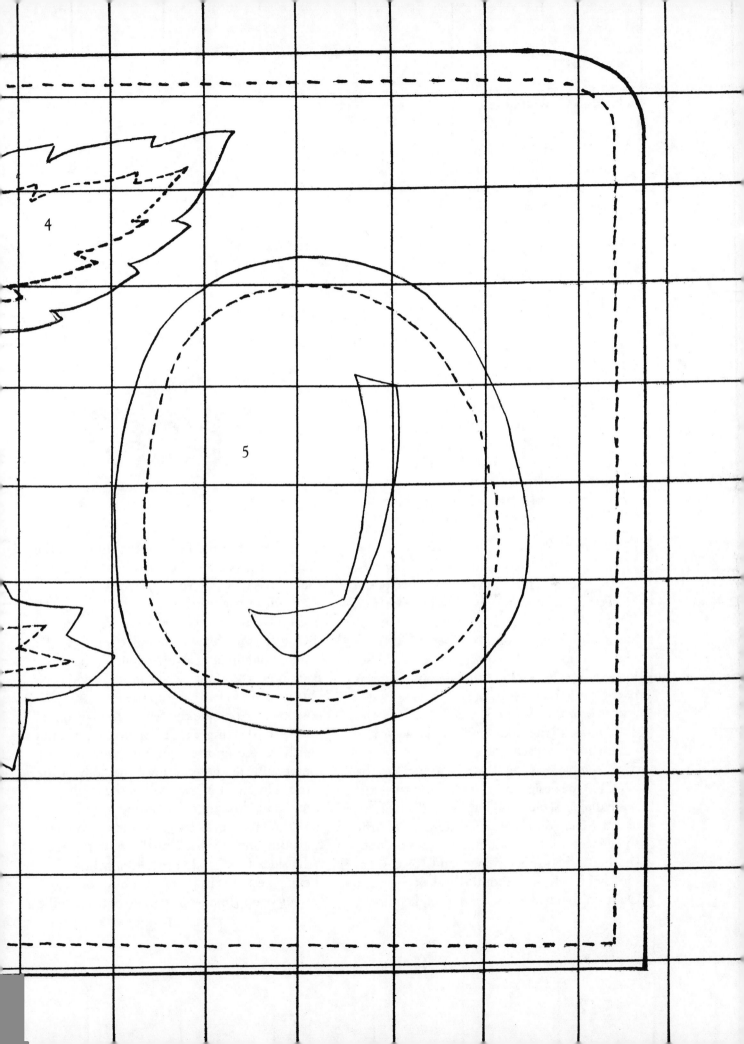

Cooking Mitts

Always a useful addition to any kitchen, cooking mitts are easy to make and fun to look at if you put colorful designs on them. Here are two ideas—a turtle and a girl with a flowerpot. Remember to quilt the mitt before you appliqué the designs.

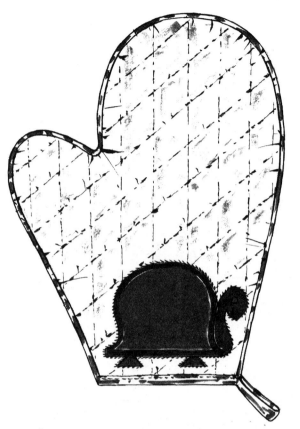

Turtle

Size:
6½ x 9 inches

Materials:
½ yard of plain-colored material, 36 inches
    wide, for the front and the back of the mitt
Scraps of material for the turtle design
½ yard of lining material, 36 inches wide
Small roll of batting
Small amount of loose polyester stuffing
Bias tape

Directions:
1. Make a template for the mitt. Using this, cut two pieces of the plain material, two pieces of batting and two pieces of lining material. Remember to reverse the template when you are marking the second outline on both the plain fabric and the lining material. Also, make templates for the turtle design. Cut one of the turtle body (#1), one of the shell (#2) and two of the feet (#3).
2. Cut out all the pieces and transfer seam and accent lines to each piece.
3. Assemble and quilt the mitt before you appliqué the design on its side. To do this, first mark diagonal quilting lines on both the front and the back of the mitt. Next, assemble the three layers for the front of the mitt—the top, the batting and the lining—and baste them together. Do the same for the back of the mitt. Quilt on the marked quilting lines, beginning in the center of the front of the mitt. Do the same for the back of the mitt. Set the back of the mitt aside while you appliqué the turtle to the front of the mitt.
4. Appliqué the shell (#2) onto the body of the turtle (#1), leaving a small opening at the top for stuffing later. Now appliqué the turtle body onto the front of the mitt, leaving the bottom open so you can slip the feet (#3) into position. Appliqué the feet at the bottom of the turtle, leaving a small opening, and stuff lightly. Close up the opening. Now close up the opening at the bottom of the body of the turtle. Finally, stuff the shell of the turtle very firmly and close up the opening.
5. When the turtle design is completed, baste the front and the back of the mitt together, right sides facing, along the seam line. Sew them together, either by machine or hand, leaving open 2 inches along the bottom of the

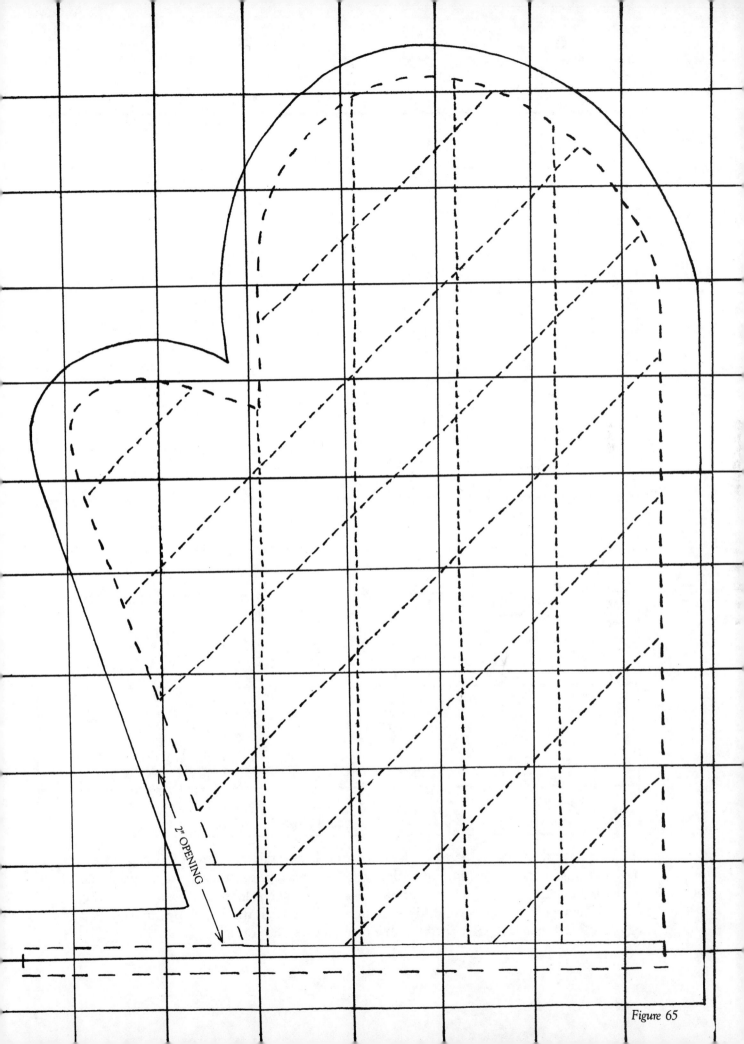

2" OPENING

Figure 65

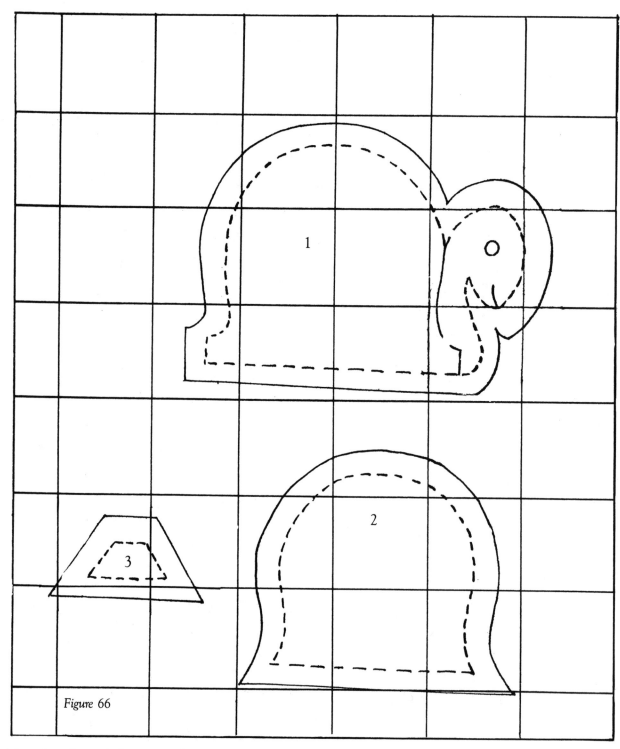

Figure 66

thumb side and the entire bottom edge. Remove bastings and turn the mitt right side out.
6. Baste bias tape along the bottom edges and extend the tape 2 inches beyond the bottom edge on the thumb side. Sew the bias tape in place, and then sew the open edges of the excess tape together. Form the excess tape into a hanging loop and sew it to the mitt. Whipstitch the 2-inch opening closed and remove all bastings.

Girl with a Flowerpot

Size:
6½ x 9 inches

Materials:
½ yard of plain-colored material, 36 inches wide, for the front and back of the mitt
Scraps of plain-colored and print material
½ yard of lining material, 36 inches wide
Small roll of batting
Small amount of loose polyester stuffing
Bias tape

Directions:
1. Make a template for the mitt. Cut two pieces of the plain material, two pieces of batting and two pieces of lining material. Remember to reverse the template when you are marking the second outline on both the plain fabric and the lining material. Also, make templates for the six different parts of the girl with a flowerpot. You will need to cut one of the hair (#1), one of the head (#2), one of the body (#3), one of the flower (#4), three of the leaf (#5) and one of the flowerpot (#6).
2. Cut out all the pieces and transfer seam and accent lines to each piece.
3. Assemble and quilt the mitt before you appliqué the design on its side. To do this, first mark diagonal quilting lines on both the front and the back of the mitt. Next, assemble the three layers for the front of the mitt—the top, the batting and the lining—and baste them together. Do the same for the back of the mitt. Quilt on the marked quilting lines, beginning in the center of the front of the mitt. Do the same for the back of the mitt. Set the back of the mitt aside while you appliqué the design to the front of the mitt.
4. Before beginning to appliqué, embroider the eyes and the mouth on the head (#2). Use French knots for the eyes and a chain stitch for the mouth. For the accent lines on the flower (#4), use a satin stitch or several large French knots.

Appears in color on page 37

5. Now appliqué the body (#3) on the front of the mitt. Appliqué the head (#2) next and then the hair (#1). Now appliqué the flowerpot (#6) in place, leaving the top open in order to slip the leaves into place. After appliquéing the leaves in position, close the opening at the top of the pot. Now appliqué the flower (#4) in place, leaving an opening for stuffing. Stuff the flower quite fully and close up the opening. Embroider the bows on the top of the hair (#1) with the satin stitch. If you wish to have more leaves in the flowerpot, as shown in the illustration above, embroider several, using the satin stitch. If you used plain material for the girl's body, you could add stripes by embroidering the chain stitch in rows, as shown in the illustration.
6. When you have completed the design, baste the front and the back of the mitt to-

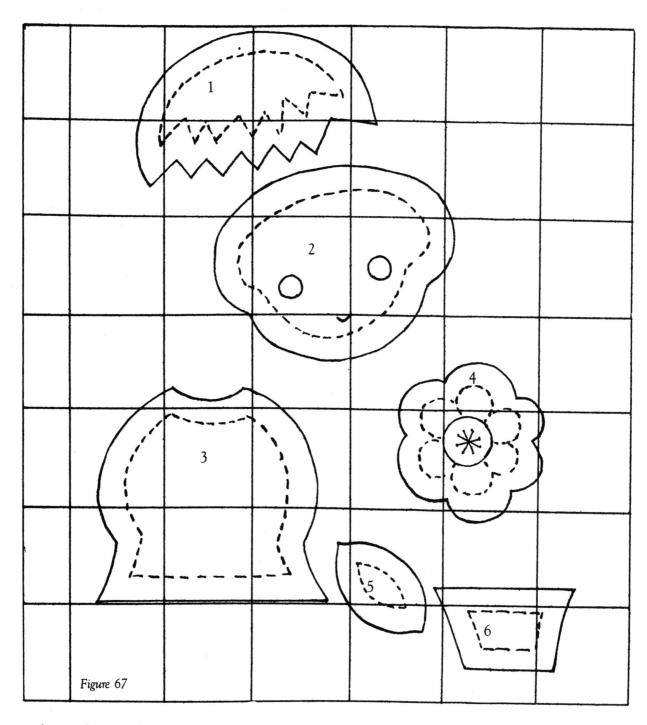

Figure 67

gether, right sides facing, along the seam line. Sew them together, either by hand or machine, leaving open 2 inches along the bottom of the thumb side and the entire bottom edge. Remove bastings and turn the mitt right side out.

7. Baste bias tape along the bottom edges and extend the tape 2 inches beyond the bottom edge on the thumb side. Sew the bias tape in place, then sew the open edges of the excess tape together. Form the excess tape into a hanging loop and sew it to the mitt. Whipstitch the 2-inch opening closed and remove all bastings.

Pot Holders

Because you can never have too many homemade pot holders, I am giving seven different designs from which you can choose. Except for the first one, which is a rain hex sign, all are adapted from old quilt patterns. Pot holders are another good way to use up scraps of material, but if you are making any for gifts, you might like to buy fabric in special colors or prints to make them more attractive.

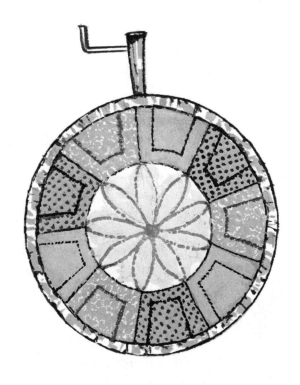

Wheel

Size:
9 inches in diameter

Materials:
½ yard of plain-colored material, 36 inches wide, for the inner circle and backing

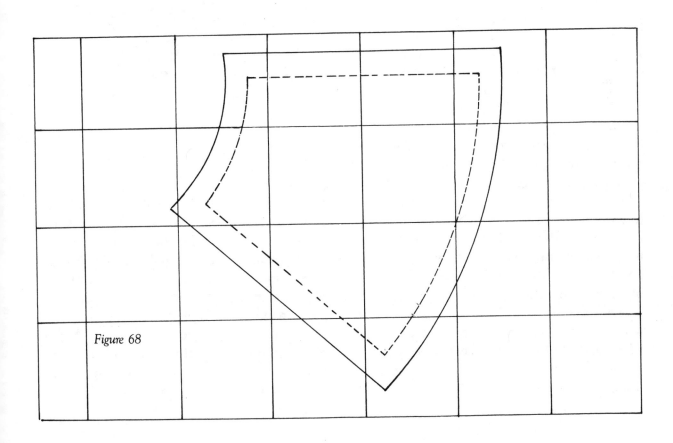

Figure 68

Scraps of plain-colored and print material
Small piece of batting
Bias tape
Plastic ring, 1 inch

Directions:

1. Make a template for the outside spoke (#1). You will need to cut nine of the outside spokes from a variety of scraps. Transfer seam lines to each piece.

2. Piece the nine outside spokes (#1) along the straight sides until you complete the wheel. Press all seams open.

3. To cut the inner circle, place the pieced wheel on top of the plain fabric and trace the outline of the inner circle. Remove the wheel, add a ¼-inch seam allowance on the edge of the marked circle and cut it out.

4. Appliqué the pieced spokes to the outside edge of the inner circle.

5. Mark the quilting lines on the completed top. Check the illustration on page 165 carefully and note the curved lines on the inner circle. These are quilting lines. To duplicate them on your top, find the exact center of the inner circle and mark it. Draw a line from the center to the bottom of each seam, bowing it slightly, as in the illustration, to get the desired effect. Now mark quilting lines about ¼ inch inside all the outside spokes.

6. To cut the backing, place the completed top face down on the plain fabric and trace around its outer edges. Mark the ¼-inch seam allowance. Cut out the backing. Do the same to cut out the batting.

7. Baste together the top, batting and backing. Begin quilting in the center first, and then do the lines in the outside spokes.

8. Trim off any excess batting. Baste the bias tape first to the front edge of the pot holder and whipstitch in place. Then turn the tape to the back edge, thus encasing the raw edges, and whipstitch in place. Sew the plastic ring onto the bias tape securely.

Dresden Plate

Size:
10-inch square

Materials:
½ yard of plain-colored material, 36 inches wide, for top and backing
Scraps of plain-colored and print material
Small piece of batting
Plastic ring, 1 inch

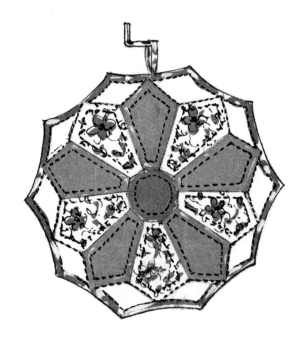

Directions:

1. Make templates for each of the two different parts of the design. Mark on each how many pieces to cut and from which fabric. You will need to cut five of the outside point (#1) out of plain scraps, five of the outside point (#1) out of print scraps and one of the center piece (#2) out of plain fabric. Transfer seam lines to each piece. You will also need to cut two 10½-inch squares out of the plain fabric and one 10½-inch square from the batting. Mark a ¼-inch seam allowance on all the squares.

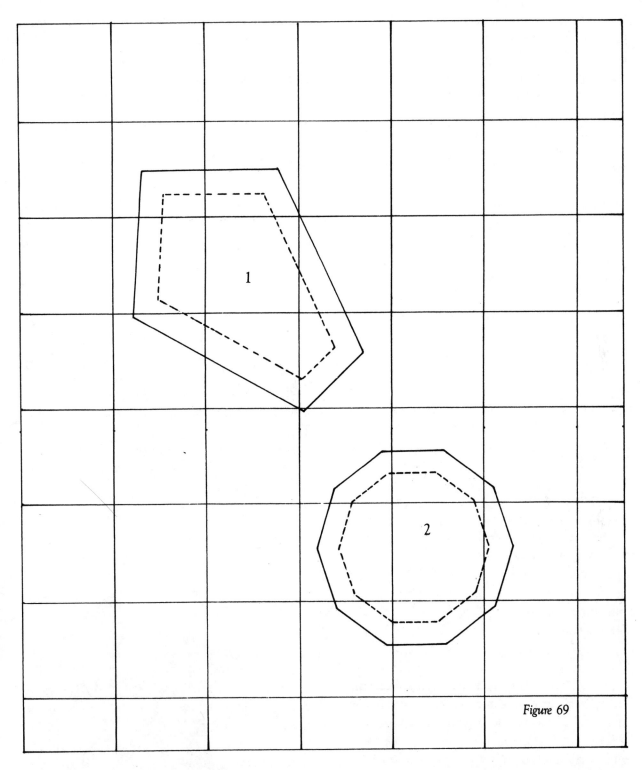

Figure 69

2. Study the illustration on page 166 to see how the outside points fit together. Piece them, alternating print and plain material, always working from the top down on each seam. When they are all pieced, appliqué them to the center of the top of the pot holder, as

shown. Now appliqué the center piece (#2) to the pot holder, making sure its edges cover the bottom edges of the outside points (#1).

3. Mark the quilting lines ¼ inch from each seam line on #1 and #2 and also the outside outline of the plate.

4. Baste together the top, the batting and the backing of the pot holder. Begin quilting in the center of the top, and continue until all quilting lines are completely stitched.

5. You can now either leave the pot holder square or trim it, as shown in the illustration, cutting it so a point lands between each point of the plate. Trim off any excess batting. Fold under the seam allowances on both the top and the backing and whipstitch together. Sew the plastic ring to the pot holder.

Eight-Pointed Star

Size:
7 inches in diameter

Materials:
¼ yard of plain-colored material, 36 inches wide, for the top and backing
Scraps of material for the design
Small piece of batting
Small amount of loose polyester stuffing
Bias tape
Plastic ring, 1 inch

Directions:
1. Make templates for each of the three different parts of the design. Mark on each how many pieces to cut and from which fabric. You will need to cut eight of the small point (#1), four of the arch center piece (#2) and one of the large center point (#3). Transfer seam lines to each piece. You will also need to cut two circles with 7½-inch diameters from the plain material and one from the batting. Mark a ¼-inch seam allowance on all the circles.

2. Study the illustration below to see how the three different shapes fit together. First, appliqué the center point (#3) in the middle of the top. Leave a small opening on one side to stuff later. Next, appliqué the four arch center pieces (#2), making sure they fit into the curves of the center (#3). Finally, appliqué the small points (#1) on the curves of the arch pieces (#2). Leave openings on the sides of the points for stuffing. Now stuff the center point (#3) and all the #1 points lightly. Close up all the openings.

3. Mark the quilting lines, following an outline pattern around each part of the design.

4. Baste together the top, the batting and the backing of the pot holder. Begin quilting around the center point first, and then around the rest of the shapes.

5. Trim off any excess batting. Baste the bias tape first to the front edge of the pot holder and whipstitch in place. Then turn the tape to the back edge, thus encasing the raw edges, and whipstitch in place. Sew the plastic ring onto the bias tape securely.

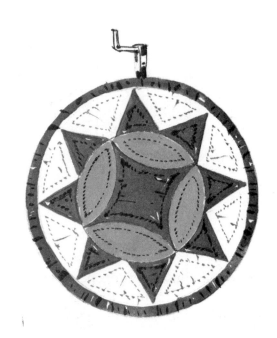

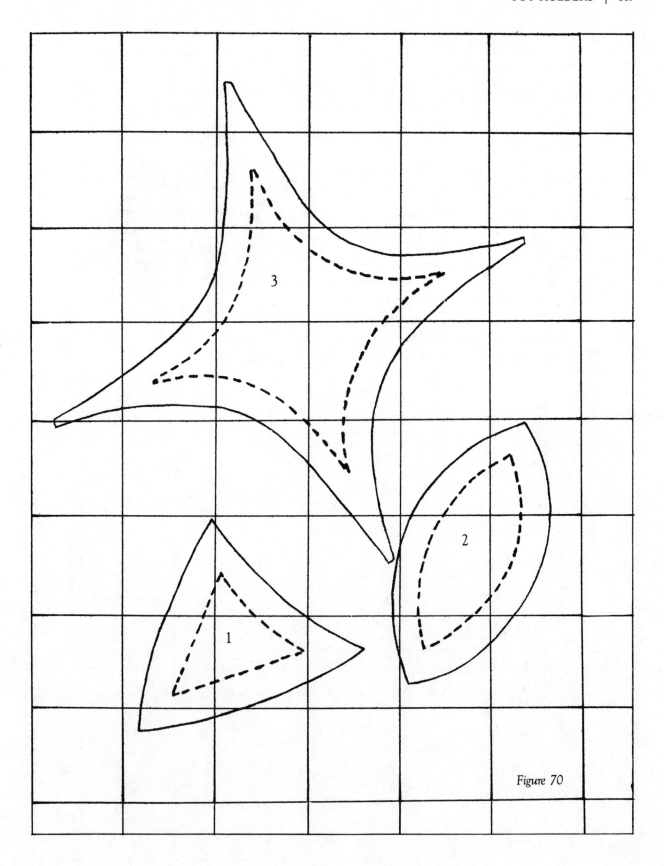

Figure 70

Flower

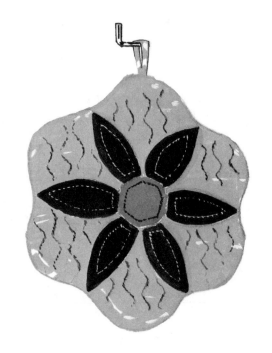

Size:

9 inches in diameter

Materials:

½ yard of plain-colored material, 36 inches
   wide, for the top and backing
Scraps of material for the design
Small piece of batting
Small amount of loose polyester stuffing
Plastic ring, 1 inch

Directions:

1. Make templates for the two different parts
of the design. Mark on each how many pieces
to cut and from which fabric. You will need to
cut six of the petal (#1) and one of the center
piece (#2). Transfer seam lines to each piece.

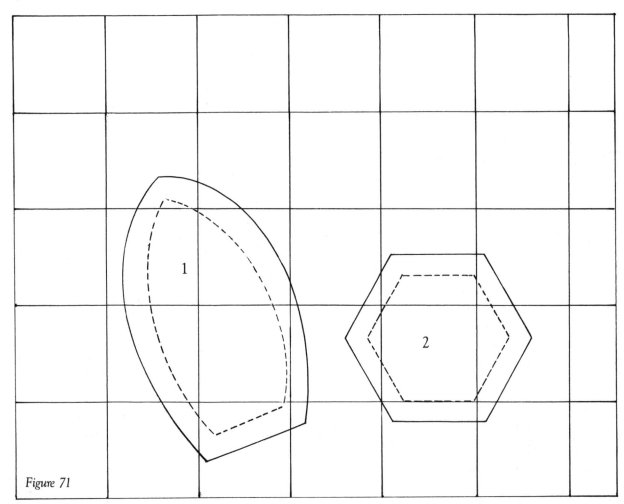

Figure 71

You will also need to cut two circles, 9½ inches in diameter each, out of the plain fabric and one circle, 9½ inches in diameter, out of the batting. Mark a ¼-inch seam allowance on all the circles.

2. Study the illustration on page 170 to see how to appliqué the petals. They must be near enough to the center that the center piece (#2) will touch all lower edges. Appliqué the petals in place, leaving an opening on the side of each petal for stuffing later. Appliqué the center piece (#2). Now stuff each petal lightly and close up the openings.

3. Mark quilting lines, outlining the petals and the inside of the center piece. The rest of the open space can be marked with wavy lines, as shown in the illustration.

4. Baste the top, batting and backing of the pot holder together. Begin quilting in the center of the top, and continue until all lines have been completely stitched.

5. Trim off any excess batting. Use a round object such as a bowl or plate to guide you when marking the scalloped edge, as shown in the illustration. Trim the marked edge, and then fold under the seam allowance on both the top and the backing. Whipstitch the folded edges together. Sew the plastic ring securely to the holder.

Rain Hex Sign

Size:
7 inches in diameter

Materials:
¼ yard plain-colored material, 36 inches wide, for the top and backing
Scraps of material for the design
Small piece of batting
Small amount of loose polyester stuffing
Bias tape
Plastic ring, 1 inch

Directions:
1. Make templates for each of the three different parts of the design. Mark on each how many pieces to cut and from which fabric. You will need to cut four raindrops (#1), one small circle (#2) and one larger center circle (#3). Transfer seam lines to each piece. Also cut two circles with 7½-inch diameters from the plain fabric and one from the batting. Mark a ¼-inch seam allowance on each of the three circles.

2. Study the illustration below to see the position of each raindrop. Appliqué all four raindrops (#1) in place, leaving a small opening on the top of each for stuffing. Stuff lightly and close up the openings. Now appliqué the larger center circle (#3) in the exact center of the top. Appliqué the small circle (#2) in the center of the larger circle. Leave an opening and stuff it lightly. Close up the opening.

3. Mark quilting lines, following the outline of each raindrop and the circle in the center. The remaining open space can be filled with wavy lines, as shown in the illustration.

4. Baste together the top, the batting and the backing of the pot holder. Begin quilting around the center first, and then around each raindrop. Do the background quilting last.

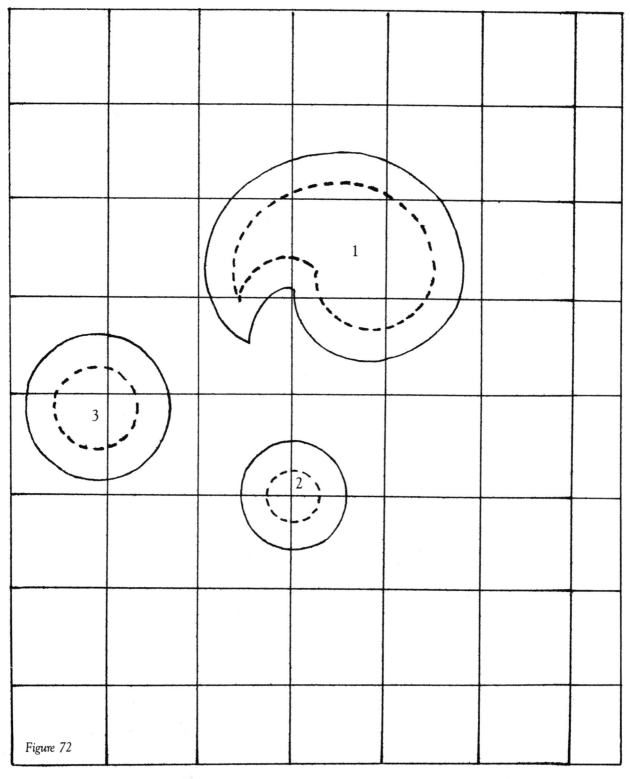

Figure 72

5. Trim off any excess batting. Baste the bias tape to the front edge of the pot holder and whipstitch in place. Then turn the tape to the back edge, thus encasing the raw edges, and whipstitch in place. Sew the plastic ring onto the bias tape securely.

Fan

Size:
8 inches square

Materials:
¼ yard of plain-colored material, 36 inches
   wide, for the top and backing
Scraps of material for the design
Small piece of batting
Bias tape
Plastic ring, 1 inch

Directions:
1. Make templates for each of the three different parts of the design. Mark on each how
many pieces to cut and from which fabric. You
will need to cut five of the center piece (#1),
one of the base point (#2) and five of the

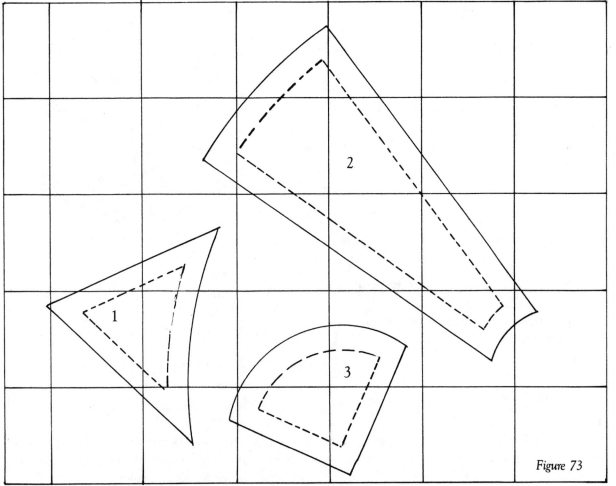

Figure 73

outside point (#3). Transfer seam lines to each piece. You will also need to cut two 8½-inch squares out of the plain fabric and one 8½-inch square from the batting. Mark a ¼-inch seam allowance on all the squares.

2. Piece the five parts of the center piece (#1) together, checking the illustration on page 173 to see how they fit together. Appliqué them to the center of the square as shown. Now appliqué the base point (#2) to the bottom. Finally, appliqué all the outside points (#3) to the top of the center piece.

3. Mark quilting lines, following the outline of the fan as shown in the illustration. For the rest of the white space, you can repeat the outline.

4. Baste together the top, the batting and the backing of the pot holder. Begin quilting in the center first and continue until all quilting lines are completely stitched.

5. Trim off any excess batting. Baste your bias tape first to the front edge of the pot holder and whipstitch in place. Then turn the tape to the back edge, thus encasing the raw edges, and whipstitch in place. Sew the plastic ring onto the bias tape securely.

Six-Pointed Star

Size:
8 inches square

Materials:
¼ yard of print material, 36 inches wide, for the top and backing
Scraps of plain-colored material in two different colors
Small piece of batting
Bias tape
Plastic ring, 1 inch

Directions:
1. Make templates for the two different parts of the design. Mark on each how many pieces to cut and from which fabric. You will need to cut six large points (#1) from one plain fabric and six small points (#2) from another plain fabric. Transfer seam lines to each piece. You will also need to cut two 8½-inch squares from the print material and one 8½-inch square from the batting. Mark a ¼-inch seam allowance on all the squares.

2. Study the illustration below to see how the parts fit together. Appliqué the small points (#2) first, making sure all the bottoms touch, thus forming the center. Now appliqué the large points (#1), fitting them to the sides of the small points.

3. Mark quilting lines, outlining each piece both inside and outside all seam lines. The rest of the open space can be filled with straight lines.

4. Baste together the top, the batting and the backing of the pot holder. Begin quilting in the center first, and continue quilting until all lines are completely stitched.

5. Note on the illustration how the square has been cut to form six points. Cut your top, batting and backing this way. Trim off any

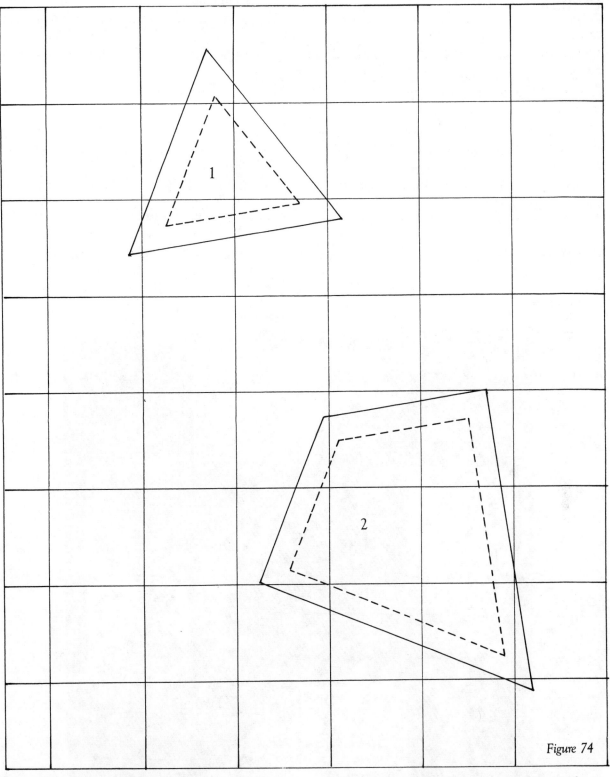

Figure 74

excess batting. Baste your bias tape to the front edge of the pot holder and whipstitch in place. Then turn the tape to the back edge, thus encasing the raw edges, and whipstitch in place. Sew the plastic ring onto the bias tape securely.

Plate Mats

Here are two designs for plate mats. You could easily make a backing out of a single piece of fabric simply by tracing the outline of the completed top instead of using the pieced backing. These are also good designs to use on place mats. If you want to change their size, appliqué the completed design onto a piece of plain fabric cut to the proper dimensions for your table, and use these larger dimensions to cut your backing and batting.

Star of the West

Size:
10 inches square

Materials:
¼ yard of light print material, 36 inches wide
¼ yard of dark print material, 36 inches wide
Small piece of batting
Bias binding

Directions:
1. Make templates for each of the three different parts of the design. Mark on each how many pieces to cut and from which fabric. If you are piecing both the top and the back, you will need to cut eight of the square (#1) from the dark print fabric, eight of the square (#1) from the light print, eight of the triangle (#2) from the light print, eight of the triangle (#2) from the dark print and eight of the diamond (#3) from the dark print. Transfer seam lines

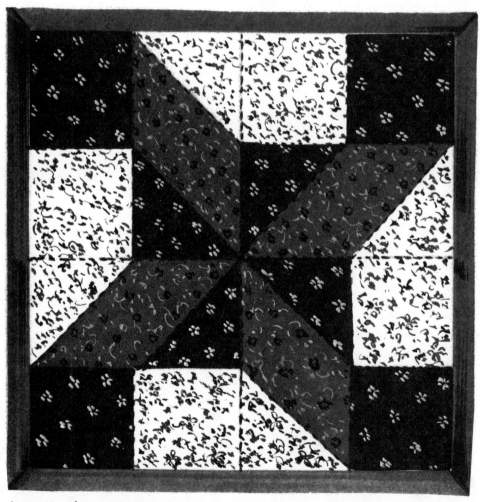

Appears in color on page 37

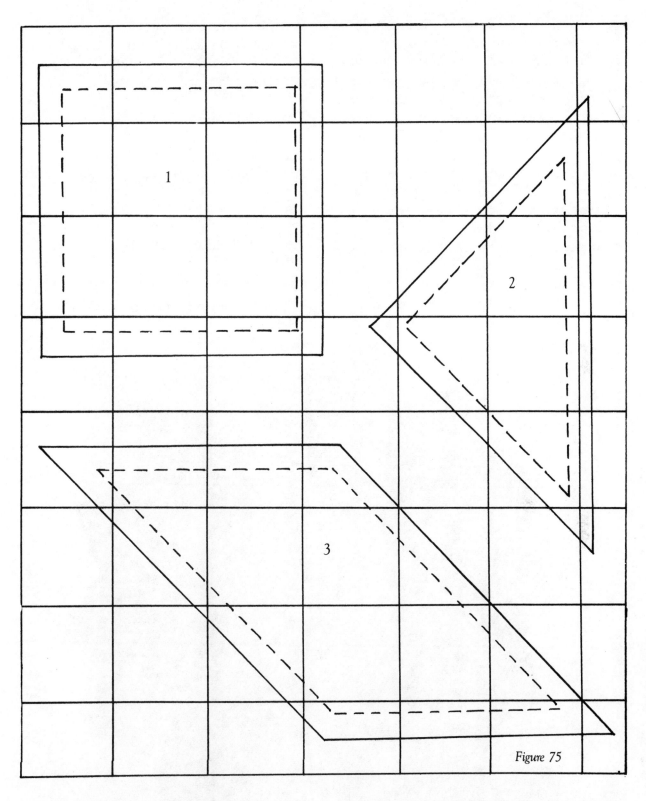

Figure 75

to each piece. Also, cut a square piece of batting measuring 10½ inches.

2. To make the top, begin piecing at the center and work out. Check the illustration opposite to see how the various pieces fit together. First, join the triangles (#2) cut from the dark

print to the long side of the diamonds (#3). Next, join—on all sides—the squares (#1) and the triangles (#2) that were both cut from the light print. Finally, add the squares (#1) cut from the dark print to each corner. Press seams open. Following the same sequence, piece the back of the plate mat. Press seams open.

3. Mark quilting lines on the top by measuring ¼ inch from all the lines on both sides.

4. Baste the three layers—the top, the batting and the back—together.

5. Begin quilting in the center of the top, and continue until all marked lines are completely stitched.

6. Trim off excess batting. Baste the bias tape to the front edge of the plate mat and whipstitch in place. Then turn the tape to the back edge, thus enclosing the raw edges, and whipstitch in place.

Dresden Plate

Size:
Approximately 14 inches in diameter

Materials:
A selection of large scraps of both plain-colored and print material
Small piece of batting

Directions:
1. Make a template for the petal (#1). You will

Appears in color on page 37

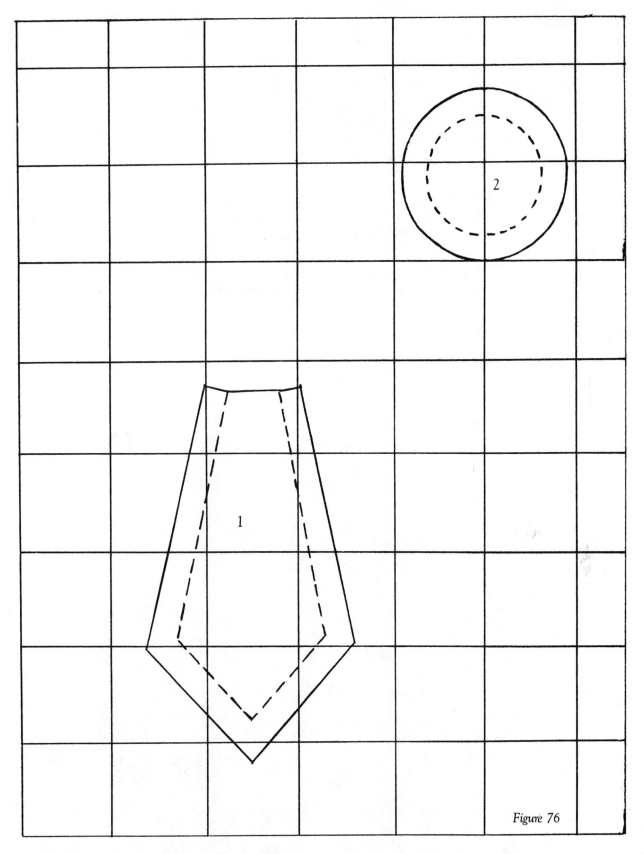

Figure 76

need to cut fourteen of the petal from the print scraps for the top and fourteen of the petal from the plain scraps for the back. Transfer seam lines to each piece.

2. Begin piecing the top of the plate by joining the fourteen print petals at their sides, thus forming a circle. Do the same for the fourteen petals cut from plain scraps for the back.

3. Place the completed circle face down flat on a piece of fabric that is larger than its open center. Mark the center, and then remove the pieced circle. Now mark a circle (#2) that is ¼ inch larger and add a ¼-inch seam allowance. Do the same for the back. Now appliqué these center circles to both the top and the back, making sure that all the bottom ends of the petals are covered by the circles' edges.

4. Mark quilting lines on the top about ¼ inch inside each petal and the center. Fill in the rest of the center with smaller circles.

5. Place the top down on a piece of batting and trace around it. Cut out the batting. Baste the three layers—the print top, the batting and the plain back—together securely.

6. Begin quilting in the center, and continue until all the marked lines are completely stitched.

7. Trim off any excess batting and fold under the raw edges of both the top and back. Whipstitch them neatly together.

7. Designs for Classic Quilts

Victoria Green Quilt

This 1850 quilt design was originally created to honor Queen Victoria; hence the name. Because it is often done in red and green and the large flower resembles a snowflake, it is traditionally made and given at Christmas. I like to finish the edges by attaching a bright green or red contrasting border.

Size:
70 x 70 inches
Twenty-five 14-inch blocks, 5 across and 5 down

Materials:
5 yards of white or off-white material, 36 inches wide, for the top background blocks
4½ yards of white or off-white material, 36 inches wide, for the backing and the flower centers and petals
2½ yards of red material, 36 inches wide, for the flowers
2 yards of green material, 36 inches wide, for the leaves
Large roll of batting
Small amount of loose polyester stuffing
Red or green bias binding (optional)

Directions:
1. Make templates for each of the four parts of the design and mark on each how many to cut and from which fabric. You will need to cut 100 of the flower (#1) from the red fabric and 300 of the leaf (#2) from the green fabric. You will need 800 of the petal (#3) and 100 of the flower center (#4), both cut from the same fabric as that used for the top background blocks.
2. Cut out twenty-five 14½-inch squares from the top background material. Mark a ¼-inch seam allowance on each.
3. Cut out all the design pieces and transfer seam and accent lines to each piece. Stack them in piles according to shape and color.
4. Appliqué the petals and centers (#3 and #4) onto the flowers (#1).
5. Study the illustration on page 182—it shows one complete block—and note the arrangement of the flowers and leaves. Appliqué all the flowers in place first. Next, appliqué the leaves. If you want to stuff them—and I think they look better stuffed lightly—leave a small opening. Use a long darning needle or a small knitting needle and push the stuffing around until it is evenly distributed and firm. Close up the openings.
6. Finish appliquéing and stuffing each block completely before beginning the next.
7. When all blocks are completed, lay them on a flat surface in rows of five across and five down. Baste the blocks together along the seam lines, making sure that all corners meet

Appears in color on page 38

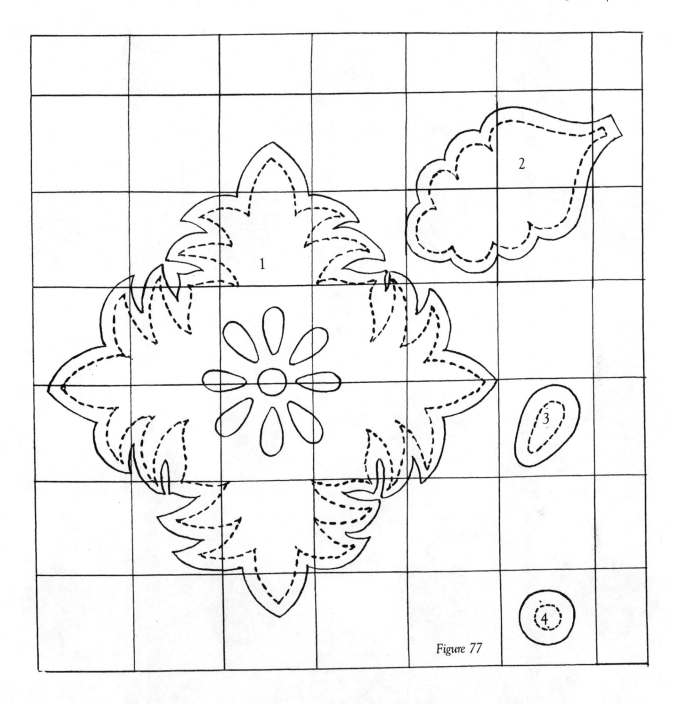

Figure 77

exactly. Sew them together either by hand or machine, and remove the bastings. Press all seams open.

8. Mark the quilting lines on the completed top. I suggest using an outline pattern around the leaves and flowers and straight diagonal lines in the open spaces.

9. Cut and piece the backing to the proper size. Cut the batting to the proper size. Baste all three layers—the completed top, the batting and the backing—together securely.

10. Begin quilting through the center of the top, and continue until all quilting lines have been stitched completely.

11. Finish the raw edges by adding a contrasting border of bias binding.

Appears in color on front cover

Strawberry Quilt

This delightful quilt was first made during the 1800s. Although it uses the traditional red and green colors, there is no reason why you could not choose others. In fact, in the South, the same design, made in brown and green calicoes, was given the name Tobacco Leaf. In the countryside when the sides of the huge tobacco barns were lifted on their hinges to allow the leaves to dry, it was said that they looked like a succession of giant quilts.

This design is a perfect one for stuffing. I stuff both the stems and the strawberries. I have sometimes used plain red material for the berries and then embroidered the seeds on them, but you can use a printed fabric—calico or paisley—with a red background to create the same effect with much less effort. I think a self-binding is your best bet for finishing the edges, but if you wish you could use either a red or green contrasting border.

Size:
80 x 90 inches
Seventy-two 10-inch blocks, 8 across and 9 down

Materials:
7¼ yards of white or off-white material, 36 inches wide, for the top background blocks
9 yards of white or off-white material, 36 inches wide, for the backing
3 yards of red printed material, 36 inches wide, for the strawberries
3 yards of green material, 36 inches wide, for the leaves and stems
Large roll of batting
Small amount of loose polyester stuffing
Bias binding (optional)

Directions:
1. Make a template for each of the six different parts of the design and mark on each how many to cut and from which fabric. You will need to cut 1,296 berries (#1) from the red printed fabric. You will need 360 long straight stems (#2), 360 long curved stems (#3), 1,440 leaves (#4), 432 short curved stems (#5) and 144 short stems for the single strawberry (#6), all cut from the green fabric.
2. Cut out seventy-two 10½-inch squares from the top background material. Mark a ¼-inch seam allowance on each.
3. Cut out all the design pieces and transfer seam lines to each piece. Stack them in piles according to shape and color.
4. Study the illustration opposite—it shows one complete block—and note the placement of all parts of the design, particularly the single strawberries.
5. Appliqué the long, straight stems (#2) in place first and leave an opening at the top. If you wish to stuff them, use a long knitting needle and distribute the stuffing evenly down the entire length of the stem. Do not close up the top opening now, as you will want to tuck the bottom of the strawberry underneath it later.
6. Next, appliqué the long curved stems (#3) and the short curved stems (#5) on the sides of the stems. Leave an opening at the wide end to tuck the strawberry in place. You might like to stuff these shorter stems just a little. If so, do it now, but do not close up the opening. Appliqué the leaves (#4) on both stems; I would not stuff them.
7. Now appliqué the strawberries (#1) in place, tucking the wide ends of the berries under the loose ends of the stems. Leave an opening at the side of each berry for stuffing. Stuff them all quite firmly and close up all openings.
8. Next, appliqué the single strawberries in place. Leave an opening at the side of each, and stuff them quite firmly. Close up the opening. Appliqué the short straight stems (#6) onto the bottoms of the single strawberries, so that their wide ends overlap the bottoms of the berries. Stuff them if you wish.
9. Finish appliquéing and stuffing each block

completely before beginning the next.

10. When all the blocks for the top are finished, lay them in rows of eight across and nine down on a flat surface. Baste the blocks together along the seam lines, making sure all corners meet exactly. Sew the blocks together, either by hand or machine, and remove the bastings. Press all seams open.

11. Mark the quilting lines on the assembled top. I suggest an outline pattern around all the design pieces and additional curved lines (see illustration on page 22) for the open spaces.

12. Cut and piece the backing to the required size. Cut the batting to the proper size. Baste the three layers—the completed top, the batting and the backing—together securely.

13. Begin quilting through the center of the top, and continue until all quilting lines have been stitched completely.

14. Finish the raw edges either by self-binding or by adding a contrasting border of bias binding.

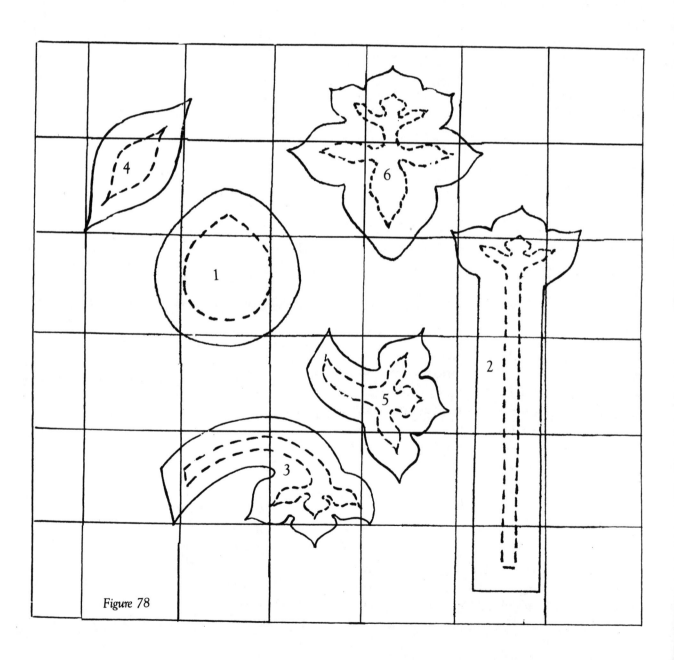

Figure 78

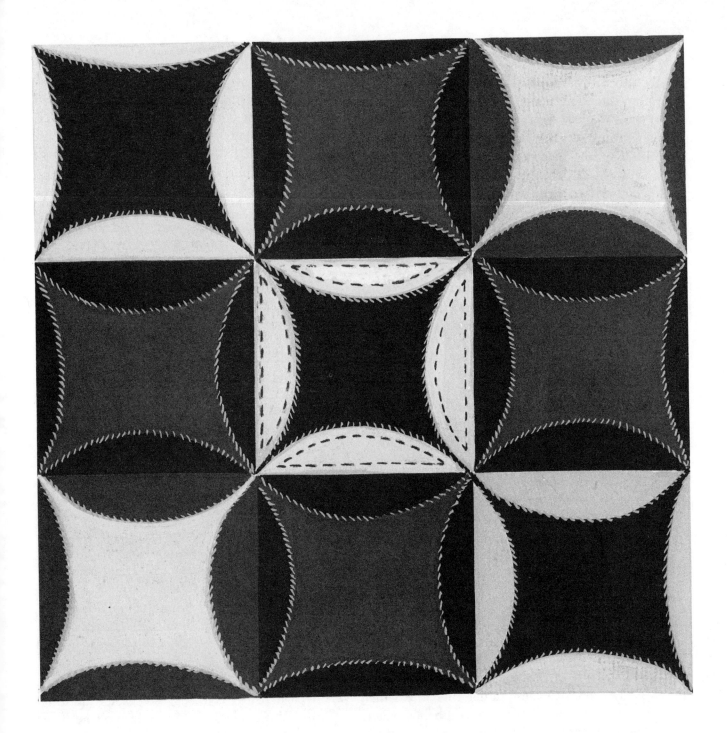

Rob Peter to Pay Paul Quilt

This quilt is so named because the center pieces are cut out to add to the sides, while the side pieces appear trimmed to fill out the centers. The final effect looks like a series of cir-

cles, but actually each unit is a perfect square. The trick to creating this marvelous design is picking out the three colors and planning their layout beforehand. I have selected three rather somber colors—black, gray and tan—but you could easily select others, one of which might be a print rather than a plain color. The important thing is to work out their placement. In my directions I include a detailed plan showing how to piece each square and how to alternate the blocks when you join them to form the quilt top. You can easily substitute different-colored centers and sides, but make sure you have the right number of each. Do all your calculations before cutting out the fabrics. Since this is an entirely pieced quilt top, it is essential that all seam joinings be as nearly accurate as possible so as not to destroy the wonderful optical illusion. To finish the edges of the quilt, I suggest simply whipstitching the folded edges together, rather than adding a border of any kind.

Size:
72 x 81 inches
Seventy-two blocks, 8 across and 9 down

Materials:
4 yards of white or off-white material, 45 inches wide, for the backing
4 yards of black material, 45 inches wide
4 yards of tan material, 45 inches wide
4 yards of gray material, 45 inches wide
Large roll of batting
Color-coordinated thread for each color of material

Directions:
1. Make a template for each of the two different parts of the design. Enlarge them by using 2-inch squares, rather than the 1-inch squares as shown. Mark on each how many pieces to cut and from what color fabric. If you are following my design, you will need to cut twenty-seven of the center (#1) from the black fabric, twenty-seven of #1 from the tan fabric and eighteen of #1 from the gray fabric. You will need to cut 108 of the side (#2) from the black fabric, 108 of #2 from the gray fabric and seventy-two of #2 from the tan fabric. Transfer seam lines to each piece.
2. Here is my plan for piecing the quilt top.

The B stands for black centers with gray sides, the G for gray centers with tan sides, and the T for tan centers with black sides.

Row 1	B T G B T G B T
Row 2	T B T G B T G B
Row 3	B T G B T G B T
Row 4	T B T G B T G B
Row 5	B T G B T G B T
Row 6	T B T G B T G B
Row 7	B T G B T G B T
Row 8	T B T G B T G B
Row 9	B T G B T G B T

Using this plan, you will piece your squares in the following way: Join four gray sides to each of the twenty-seven black centers, four tan sides to each of the eighteen gray centers, and four black sides to each of the twenty-seven tan centers. Press seams open.
3. Once you have pieced all the squares, join them according to the plan outlined above. Place them on a flat surface in the proper order, checking to see that they alternate properly. Baste them together along the seam lines and then sew them, making sure corners meet exactly. Remove bastings and press seams open.
4. Mark the quilting lines. On the illustration on page 187 I have suggested some quilting lines. You could also add more quilting lines inside each center, following its curved edges.
5. Cut and piece the backing to the proper size. Cut the batting to the proper size. Baste all three layers—the completed top, the batting and the backing—together securely.
6. Begin quilting through the center of the top, and continue until all quilting lines have been stitched completely.
7. Finish the raw edges by whipstitching the folded edges together.

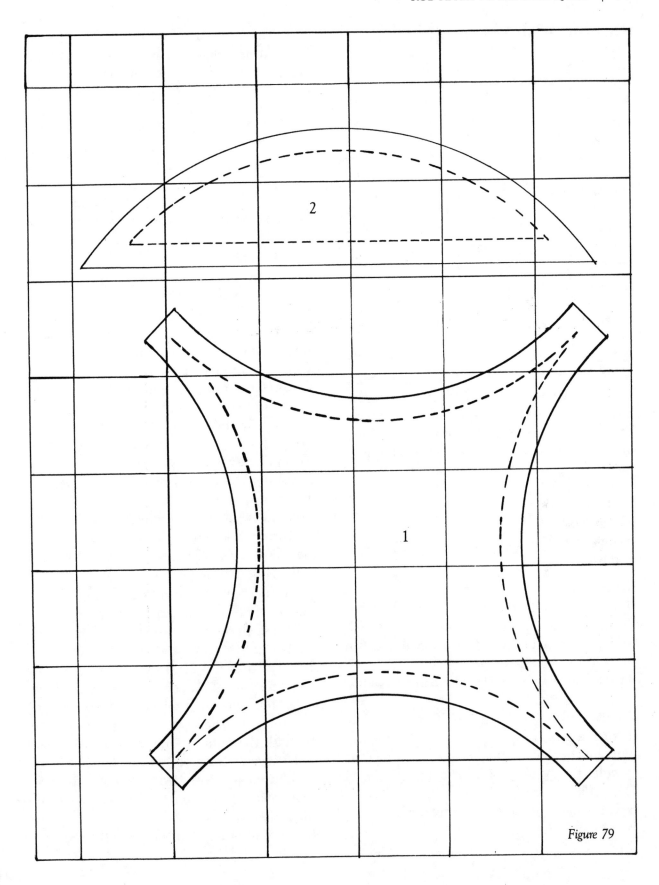

Figure 79

Double Irish Cross Quilt

The Double Irish Cross design is really just a glorified Double Irish Chain with clovers, or shamrocks if you like, appliquéd on each of the blocks. Understandably, this is said to be one of the favorite quilts of the Irish. It has also been said that if you have this quilt on your bed during a winter storm, all the snow will stay away from your front door. During the long winter months in, say, Massachusetts, this would mean it would not be such hard work in the morning to get to the barn. Who knows if it's true? But it is certainly a nice idea.

For this quilt, the small pink and green squares are first pieced together into a chain, and then the chain is appliquéd onto a block. The clovers or shamrocks are then appliquéd onto the open spaces within the chain. Self-binding is an easy way to finish the raw edges, but you might prefer to use either the green or the pink from the quilt top for a border. Both are attractive ways to finish this handsome quilt.

Size:
70 x 70 inches
Twenty-five 14-inch blocks, 5 across and 5 down

Materials:
5 yards of white or off-white material, 36 inches wide, for the top background blocks
4½ yards of white or off-white material, 36 inches wide, for the backing
3 yards of plain green material, 36 inches wide, for the green squares
2 yards of plain pink material, 36 inches wide, for the pink squares
2½ yards of green paisley material, 36 inches wide, for the shamrocks or clovers
Large roll of batting
Small amount of loose polyester stuffing
Bias binding (optional)

Directions:
1. Make templates for all three parts of the design, and mark on each how many to cut and from which fabric. You will need to cut 100 clovers with stem attached (#1) from the paisley fabric, 200 single clovers (#2) from the paisley fabric, 2,500 squares (#3) from the plain green fabric and 1,375 squares (#3) from the plain pink fabric.
2. Cut out twenty-five 14½-inch squares from the top background material. Mark a ¼-inch seam allowance on each.
3. Cut out all the design pieces and transfer seam lines to each piece. Stack them in piles according to color and shape.
4. Study the illustration opposite—it shows one complete block—to see how the squares are pieced together. Begin in the center of the chain and alternate pink and green squares, as shown. Continue joining the squares until you have finished the chain for one block, as shown. Lay the joined squares on the background block, as shown, and baste; then appliqué the chain of squares onto the block.
5. Center the clovers or shamrocks (#1) in the open spaces of the chain and appliqué in place. Leave a small opening in the clover and stuff firmly. Close the opening. Now appliqué the side clovers (#2) in place and stuff these as well. Close up the openings.
6. Finish appliquéing and stuffing each block completely before beginning on the next.
7. When all the blocks are finished, lay them in rows of five across and five down on a flat surface. Baste the blocks together along the seam lines, matching corners exactly, and then sew either by hand or machine. Remove bastings and press the seams open.
8. Mark the quilting lines on the assembled top. I suggest using an outline design around the clovers and both inside and outside each small square. Mark straight diagonal lines in all other open spaces.
9. Cut and piece the backing to the required

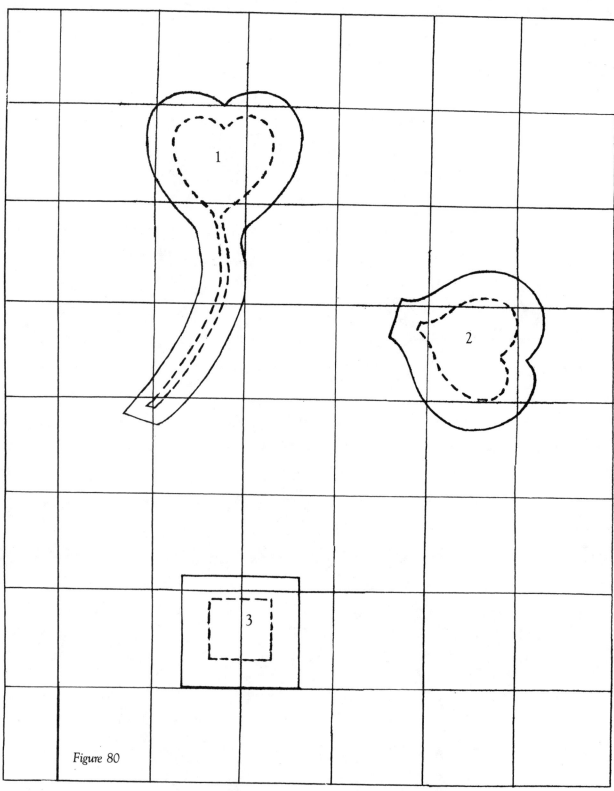

Figure 80

size. Cut the batting to the proper size. Baste the three layers—the completed top, the batting and the backing—together securely.

10. Begin quilting through the center of the top, and continue until all stitching lines have been stitched completely.

11. Finish the raw edges by self-binding or adding a contrasting border of bias binding.

Whig Rose Quilt

The design for this marvelous quilt brings to mind the early political days of our country. It is a very intricate design and requires a good deal of time and patience to make. It is both pieced and appliquéd; the handsome flower design is first appliquéd on blocks, and then the blocks are set or pieced together to form the top of the quilt. Embroidery is used to link the side flowers to the center of the design. You can easily change the colors shown in the illustration, but whatever you select, I strongly suggest a bold color for the center. As with all these classic quilts, I feel that self-binding is probably the best way to finish the edges, since it takes nothing away from the superb look of the design. However, you may wish to select one of the colors in the design and add a separate border in that color.

Size:
70 x 84 inches
Thirty 14-inch blocks, 5 across and 6 down

Materials:
6 yards of white or off-white material, 36 inches wide, for the top background blocks
5 yards of white or off-white material, 36 inches wide, for the backing
2 yards of dark red material, 36 inches wide
2 yards of light blue material, 36 inches wide
3 yards of tan material, 36 inches wide
1 yard of pink material, 36 inches wide
Embroidery floss, preferably in dark red
Large roll of batting

Directions:
1. Make a template for each of the eleven parts of the design, and mark on each how many to cut and from which fabric. You will need to cut 120 centers (#1), 120 scallop centers (#2),120 circle centers (#3), 480 of the outside petal (#4), 480 small flower centers (#5), 960 outside petals of flower (#6), 480 bud centers (#7), 960 outsides of bud (#8), 480 insides of small flower (#9), 120 pointed centers (#10) and 1,920 small leaves (#11).

2. Cut out thirty blocks, each 14½ inches square, from the top background material. Mark a ¼-inch seam allowance on each. Fold each square in half, both horizontally and vertically, and press lightly. These fold lines will help you center the design in each quarter of a block.

3. Cut out all the design pieces and transfer seam and accent lines to each piece. Stack them in piles according to shape and color.

4. All embroidery work for each block will be done after your appliquéing is completely finished. First, appliqué the pointed center (#10) to the center of the large flower center (#1). Now appliqué the circle center (#3) to the center of #10. Then appliqué the scallop center (#2) to the center of #3. Appliqué this completed center to your block. Study the illustration on page 195. This shows one complete block of the quilt. Use the fold lines as a guide to placing these centers on the block. Next, appliqué the outside petals (#4) in place around the large flower center (#1).

5. Appliqué the inside small flower (#9) to the small flower center (#5), and on each side of it appliqué the outside petal (#6). Now appliqué the assembled small flower in place on the block. Check the illustration to make sure where to put it.

6. Appliqué the outside petal of the bud (#8) to the sides of the bud center (#7). Now appliqué the buds in place on the square. Finally, appliqué the small leaves (#11) in place.

7. Do the required embroidery work. For the center of the flower (#2), work one or two large French knots. The lines from the points of the outside petal (#4) can be done in the chain stitch, and the stems connecting the leaves, buds and small flowers can be done in the stem stitch.

8. Finish all the appliqué and embroidery

Figure 81

Appears in color on page 39

work for one block before beginning the next.

9. When all the blocks are finished, lay them in rows of five across and six down on a flat surface. Baste the blocks together along the seam lines, making sure all corners meet exactly. Sew the blocks together, either by hand or machine, and remove the bastings. Press all seams open.

10. Mark the quilting lines on the assembled top. Check the illustration on page 195 for suggested outline patterns around the design, as well as for curved lines for the center of the blocks.

11. Cut and piece the backing to the required size. Cut the batting to the proper size. Baste the three layers—the completed top, the batting and the backing—together securely.

12. Begin quilting through the center of the top, and continue until all quilting lines have been stitched completely.

13. Finish the raw edges either by self-binding or by adding a contrasting border.